PROJECT KUZBAS

Other books by J.P. Morray

Pride of State
From Yalta to Disarmament
The Second Revolution in Cuba
The View from Panama
Socialism in Islam: A Study of Algeria

PROJECT KUZBAS

American Workers in Siberia (1921-1926)

by J. P. Morray

International Publishers, New York

Library of Congress Cataloging in Publication Data

Morray, J. P. (Joseph, P.), 1916–
Project Kuzbas.

Bibliography: p.
Includes index.
1. Americans—Employment—Russian S.F.S.R.—Kemerovo—
History—20th century.   2. Kemerovo (R.S.F.S.R.)—Indus-
tries—History—20th century.   I. Title.
HD8528.5.A45M67   1983   331.6′2′73047   83–12607
ISBN 0–7178–0610–3
ISBN 0–7178–0606–5 (pbk.)

*To Jessica Smith, by word
and act a teacher of
friendship now between
the USSR and the USA*

Contents

THE KUZNETSK BASIN (shaded area) in the U.S.S.R.

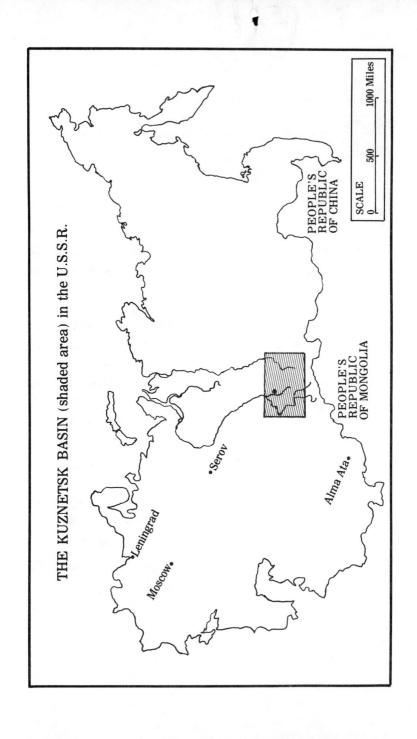

Moscow•

•Leningrad

•Serov

Alma Ata•

PEOPLE'S
REPUBLIC
OF MONGOLIA

PEOPLE'S
REPUBLIC
OF CHINA

SCALE
0   500   1000 Miles

THE KUZBAS LOCALE (shaded area of above map)

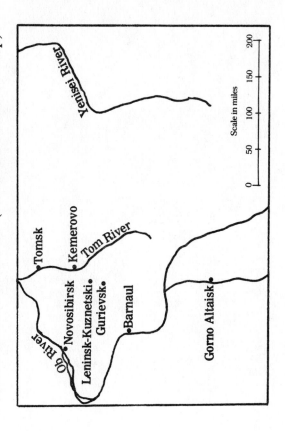

PROJECT KUZBAS

For five days during November, 1982, I had the good fortune to enjoy a rich legacy of warm feeling toward Americans that has been accumulating for sixty years in the Western Siberian city of Kemerovo, U.S.S.R. This is a very special area in the history of the American and Soviet peoples, because it was here that some five hundred Americans established an industrial colony in the early days of the Soviet Republic as a means of contributing, with their skills and experience, to the development of Soviet production in a time of desperate need. This book is a history of that colony.

The idea of founding such a colony originated in 1921 in discussions held in Moscow among two American workers, Herbert S. Calvert and William (Big Bill) Haywood, and a Dutch engineer, Sebald Rutgers. These three presented a bold plan to Lenin, who gave it his full support.

The area chosen for the location of an "autonomous industrial colony" of American workers, engineers and their families was the Kuznetsk Basin on the Tom River in Western Siberia some 2400 miles east of Moscow, about midway between Moscow and Vladivostok. The outlines of this historic initiative were embodied in an agreement negotiated between Lenin representing the Soviet Government and the "initiatory group" of American workers and the Dutch engineer.

Once the agreement was concluded, it was Herbert Calvert's assignment to return to the United States to create an American

Organization Committee and launch a campaign to recruit volunteers with the skills needed for building industry in a backward and devastated country. With a keen sense of excitement from the magnitude of the Siberian challenge and the sudden opportunity to meet it through the founding of a new international enterprise, Calvert set to work. That was in December, 1921.

Due to quirks of fate, the full history of Calvert's recruiting effort and the resulting colony that lived and worked at Kemerovo from 1922 to 1927 has never before been published. Few Americans now living have ever heard of the "Kuzbas Colony"; that is, the autonomous industrial colony in the Kuznetsk Basin. In the Fall issue of 1971, *New World Review* (New York) published a series of three articles by former colonists. These accounts made it clear that there was much drama, political and human, in this early collaboration between American and Soviet peoples which deserved full research and exposition.

With the Reagan Administration threatening to go over the brink of "cold war" to nuclear holocaust, while seeking to isolate Americans from friendly contact with the Soviet people, it seems particularly important to explore the history of this initiative from an earlier time. It should be a better known piece of our heritage. Many documents had already been assembled by Mellie Calvert, wife of Herbert Calvert, and by Ruth Epperson Kennell, a member of the Colony and a talented writer. They had planned to publish a history of Kuzbas, but unfortunately both died before it could be completed.[1] When Jessica Smith, editor emeritus of *New World Review*, asked if I would like to examine the boxes of materials in the Kennell Collection, with a view to commencing work on my own history of the Colony, I was very pleased.

An outline of the book I envisaged, together with some of the opening chapters was submitted to Novosti Publishing House in Moscow. Editors there agreed that this project promised to contribute positively to a tradition of friendship and cooperation between our two peoples and offered help in furthering my research. This included an opportunity to visit Kemerovo at the invitation of Novosti.

When I arrived in Moscow on November 15, 1982, I was met by a Novosti staff editor, Natalya G. Derevianko. She had been given the task of making all arrangements for my visit, including assembly of documents, transportation and accommodations, advance notice to local authorities and establishing contact with colonists still living in the U.S.S.R. She speaks excellent English, and I was happy to learn she would be traveling with me as research assistant and interpreter.

Thus it was that we arrived in Kemerovo in the early morning darkness after an overnight flight from Moscow aboard an Aeroflot plane. This was Siberia, and I knew that temperatures in late November could well be dropping into a range below zero Fahrenheit. Ice was beginning to form in the Tom River, and there was a foot of snow on the ground with more falling each day. Fortunately *real* winter had not yet arrived! Everyone was commenting on the mild weather and hoping, for my sake, it would last.

One of the questions I wanted to explore was, what is the importance attached to the American Kuzbas Colony in the Kemerovo consciousness of today? The welcome accorded me was a part of the answer to that question. The memory of the Colony lives in a permanent display in the local historical museum, in plaques on buildings, in the names of streets, in a monument to Sebald Rutgers, the founder who became Director of the Colony, in schoolroom history lessons, in commemorative articles in newspapers and magazines, and in research, lectures and publications at the University of Kemerovo. Everyone with whom I talked had some familiarity with the history of the Colony, and without fail, intense pleasure was expressed on learning that a book about the experience was being written for American readers. The population of Kemerovo today feels a unique bond with Americans, generated by the powerful presence of the Colony in the 1920s, an unforgettable period for the ten thousand people who then lived in Kemerovo. By their memories, by instruction, displays and other media—this valuable history is transmitted to *over a half million* people who live and work in Kemerovo today.

I was the beneficiary of that accumulated fund of memories and good will. My visit was made the occasion for several celebrations, each with something of the warmth of a reunion with old friends. We were related through a shared interest in the Colony and an agreement on its importance and value as a symbol and precedent.

The local newspaper, *Kuzbas,* with a daily circulation of 250,000, assembled some 70 reporters from the region for a press conference which focused first on the Colony but then shifted to questions about my previous books, about life in the United States, about American perceptions of the Soviet Union, about relations between the two governments. At the TV studio I was, they said, the first American ever to be interviewed on their screen. The Rector of the University of Kemerovo invited me to meet with him and several professors with a special interest in American history. This morning visit ended with a luncheon at which the conversation turned to the British–French–Israeli invasion of Egypt in 1956. We compared opinions as to why the invaders had been forced to withdraw. One Kemerovo professor stressed the importance of the Soviet ultimatum as "decisive". I attributed equal importance to a condemnation of the invasion by President Eisenhower and Secretary of State Dulles. Another professor cited votes of condemnation in the United Nations. We then agreed that the world benefited on that occasion from mutual support between the USA and the USSR in implementation of a policy with majority approval in the United Nations. We drank a toast to an instructive precedent that might well serve as a standard.

The Mayor of Kemerovo, Vladimir Veselov, received us in his office on the day of our arrival. He is a former coal miner and graduate of a technological institute in the Siberian city of Tomsk. Hearing that I wanted to learn how coal mining (a primary activity in the life of the Colony) had developed since the 1920s, he took a half-day out of his busy schedule to escort us personally to Kedrovsky, a new mining town of ten thousand people located about twenty kilometers (twelve miles) from Kemerovo. There we chatted with the mine manager, inspected the mining operation and visited some of the community facilities, including a Palace of Culture and a health resort which specializes in free preventive medical care for miners and their families.

I had also come to do research, and with Mrs. Derevianko's help and the unstinted cooperation of local libraries and museums, the next days produced much valuable material. They were willing to copy and give me anything I wanted in the way of documents and photographs. Preparation for my visit had included an advance search for materials by an experienced librarian with a special knowledge of Soviet writings about the Colony. These had been assembled for me in a tall stack with bookmarks to speed up examination and selection of those materials I wanted to have copied and added to my files.

One book displayed was a biography of Rutgers written by his daughter and son-in-law, G. and K. Trincher. It is an extremely valuable source of information about the Colony, long out of print. I had been using a copy borrowed from professor Dirk Struik, brother of Anton Struik, one of the colonists. I jokingly remarked to the librarian in Kemerovo that I might "steal" that book if not watched. She was apologetic, their only copy, etc. But at the conclusion of that working session she told me with a happy gleam that permission had been obtained from "higher authority" for the library to make me a present of their copy. It was a supreme gesture, expressive of their fervent interest in a project that would tell the story of the Kuzbas Colony to American readers.

By correspondence during the preceding months I had established contact with Professor Eugenia A. Krivosheeva of the University of Kemerovo. She has written extensively about the Colony and continues her research in the field. We were eager to meet each other for an exchange of views and information. She had had access to Soviet materials not reached by my research, and I, on the other hand, had something for her in the form of copies of documents from the Kennell Collection. "These," she said simply when I delivered them to her, "are without price."

One of the colonists, Eugene Preikshas, still lives in Kemerovo. I met with him and with two other retired coal miners, men who had worked alongside the colonists and who still enjoy recounting their impressions of the personalities and the difficulties of that eventful period. From them and from others, such as the Mayor and the Rector, I learned about the different phases in the history of Kemerovo since the 1920s.

The Colony had given impetus to a planned development that proceeded rapidly over a few decades to the emergence of a busy, modern, attractive urban center of industry, culture, parks, broad avenues and commodious apartment complexes. The production of coke and chemical by-products, which began from the work and under the conduct of the Colony, is still a major industrial activity. The oldest of these enterprises has received awards of the Order of Lenin and the Banner of Red Labor for production in crucial periods. It was a vital enterprise during the years the Nazis occupied large parts of Soviet territory west of the Urals. Metals production and manufacture use ores extracted from the region and a lumber industry draws on its forests. Coal and the chemical plants are sources of materials for the local production of nitrogen fertilizers and dyestuffs. The citizens of Kemerovo take pride in a reputation earned as a city of hard, productive workers.

Seven technical institutes study the production and construction problems of the region and prepare personnel to assume posts of work and authority. There are two higher technological institutes, two medical institutes, a culinary or food-processing institute, a music academy and two institutes devoted to literature and cultural studies. At the top of this hierarchy is the University of Kemerovo, founded in 1974. It has a faculty of 400 professors, new buildings and well-equipped laboratories.

There are also innumerable middle schools, primary schools and kindergartens. One of these last I visited and watched two- and three-year olds, under the care and tutelage of professional teachers, diligently learning how to lace boots before being bundled up in fur coats and turned out to an exuberant recess on the playgrounds.

The love of games and sports is encouraged. There are three stadiums for soccer matches and track meets, two public swimming pools, and beaches for sun-bathing and swimming in the river. There are docks and boats for recreational boating and a winter sports arena for skiing and ice-skating competitions. Cross-country skiing in the surrounding countryside is a popular pastime.

The rapid growth of the city over the past three decades has followed a plan of development, with the result that the need for space, gardens and fresh air has been served along with provision of apartment blocs, public transport and commercial establishments. I particularly enjoyed strolling along Besennaa Street, which is divided down the middle by a wide tree-lined promenade for pedestrians. At its terminus on the bank of the river stands an obelisk honoring those who gave their lives in the Great Patriotic War. (This is the phrase used in all Soviet conversation to name the war of 1941–1945). On the day I visited it, a student guard of honor in uniform, including one young woman, stood at attention around a perpetual flame. I was invited to place flowers at the base of the monument. The moment brought to mind how much we, too, owe to these honored dead.

Other statues in principal plazas of the city honor V. I. Lenin, the writer Pushkin, and Mikhail Volkov, who was the discoverer of the Kuznetsk coal seams in 1721—a balance in monuments among the political, the cultural and the productive.

The opportunities for cultural enjoyment are impressive for a city of this size. There are two theaters, one for dramatic productions and another for operettas. There are two concert halls, one the home of a philharmonic orchestra. There is a puppet theater and of course, as in so many Soviet cities, a popular circus. A dozen movie theaters show films from many different countries as well as Soviet productions.

There are four public libraries, an art gallery, a museum devoted to the history of the Kuznetsk region and another to events of the Great Patriotic War. In a museum of arts and crafts I saw an exhibition of contemporary painting done by local artists not yet ranked with those selected for display in the Art Gallery.

The development of Siberia from wasteland into advanced centers of civilized work, education and leisure, of which Kemerovo is one among many, adds enormously to the depth of Soviet resources and the security of their future. In Kemerovo it is taken for granted, but with great appreciation, that the Kuzbas Colony made a substantial contribution to the origins of this development.

An American presence continues in the libraries, where dozens of American authors in Russian editions are popular with readers. The amplified discotheque music played by a four-piece rock group with some vocals in English, some in Russian, accompanied a dance floor scene at my hotel that was hardly different from one in Denver or Chicago. Deafened by the standard decibel level of this international musical *genre*, the young people of Kemerovo were doing their mating dances like any college crowd. The authorities tolerate this influence from the bourgeois world, though not the drugs that commonly go with it in the United States. Socializing was accompanied by wine, champagne, cognac and vodka. I was told that young workers, male and female, were here mixing with young students in one of the more expensive dining and dancing restaurant-cabarets. By the end of the evening a cloud of cigarette smoke filled the room and couples were dancing somewhat closer together, just as in my home region of Portland, Oregon.

At the numerous Palaces of Culture the emphasis is on folk

dancing. I was entertained one evening by groups of young amateur dancers dressed in colorful native costumes performing spirited routines from their repertory of dances from each of the fifteen Soviet Republics. These talented young workers and children of workers highly appreciate the disciplined training they receive from professional teachers in these centers. Standards are high, and the resulting performances are brilliant, enthusiastic and surprising in their energy and precision. They are dancing to impress and please each other as well as the audience. This, too, is an opportunity for recreation, socialization and courtship. The Palaces of Culture, with strong support from the Communist Party, are holding their own against the lure of the discotheque.

Another surviving colonist whom I wanted to interview was Anna Preikshas, who was twelve years old when she arrived in Kemerovo from the United States in 1922. She had married in Siberia, become a Soviet citizen, borne children and worked in different schools and institutes as a teacher of English until her retirement in 1980. She is now living in the city of Dnepropetrovsk in the Ukraine with her daughter, who is a professor of physics at a metallurgical institute. Her health did not permit her to travel to Moscow, so in preparation for my visit Mrs. Derevianko had made arrangements for us to travel to Dnepropetrovsk, primarily to give me an opportunity to interview Anna Preikshas and examine the documents about the Colony she had collected over the years.

By the time my visit to the U.S.S.R. ended, I was weighted down with books accumulated along the way; however, these have been valuable in providing Soviet perceptions of the Colony and data on its history. My visit in Kemerovo and the conversations with Anna Preikshas added new elements to my understanding and appreciation of the exciting, turbulent, often troubled events described herein.

In the history of the Kuzbas Colony we have a shared historical experience, an early endeavor by our two peoples which was background to fruitful cooperation against the fascist Axis in World War II, against diehard European colonialists in 1956, and in joint efforts since in space exploration, and in other fields. To multiply such contacts and cooperation can only serve the security and prosperity of both our peoples.

The destinies of our two highly developed societies, the American and the Soviet, are fatefully linked. We both need to coexist peacefully in order to survive. The following account should add something to the reader's knowledge of our own history and that of the Soviet Union. It is my hope that such increased understanding will add a positive link to the chain of history that binds us together.

1

In the summer of 1921, the paths of three men came together in Moscow. Two of them, William D. Haywood and Herbert S. Calvert were Americans; the third, Sebald Rutgers, was Dutch. Given the previous history of the three in their separate spheres, it was altogether logical for each of them to find himself in Moscow in 1921 and natural for them to come together in a remarkable enterprise, the Kuzbas Colony. Its quality and destiny were bound up with the lives and character of these three principals who, with help from V. I. Lenin, gave it birth. In order better to understand the crucial events of the 1920's in which together they played decisive roles, we will begin by recounting the biography of each of the three up to the year 1921.

William D. Haywood

Bill Haywood was born of pioneering parents in Utah in 1869, when it was still a frontier region. At the age of 15 he went to work in an ore mine in Nevada. He also worked as a cowboy and as a homesteading farmer on the Nevada frontier. Hard times and loss of his farm sent him back to the mines. In Silver City, Idaho, he heard about the Western Federation of Miners, a combination of unions that aimed to bring all the miners of the West together in one organization. It was born in a bitter struggle between miners and mine-owners at the Coeur d'Alenes in Idaho. There the state governor had used Federal militia to arrest a thousand striking miners and hold them for six months in a rough-lumber barracks called the "bull pen"—without sanitation, disease-ridden, vermin-infested. Many had died.

In 1898 Haywood was elected a delegate by his local Miners' Union to a convention of the Western Federation of Miners held in Salt Lake City. There he met the men who had fought in the tragic strikes of Coeur d'Alenes, Leadville and Cripple Creek, Colorado, and there he found his own calling as a leader in class struggle. The charter of the Western Federation of Miners proclaimed: "Labor produces all wealth, wealth belongs to the producers there-of." It was consciously different from the craft unions of the American Federation of Labor headed by Samuel Gompers. The leaders of the WFM had become strong advocates of industrial unions, which would be open to all workers in an industry what-ever their craft specialty and even if they were craftless and unskilled. Also, the WFM, in contrast to the AFL, cultivated the Marxist tradition that labor for wages in a capitalist enterprise is wage-slavery.

This convention and others Haywood attended in the years following, combined with the active role he took in the many strikes of his union, molded the big, rough-hewn, warm-hearted, keen-witted westerner into one of the most ardent and effective fighters against capitalism his country has yet produced. Haywood was elected a member of the executive board of the WFM and later served many years as its Secretary-Treasurer. In his autobiography, looking back on this period, he wrote:

> These conventions had been a significant point in my life. I keenly realized the importance of the revolutionary labor movement, and now had a deeper understanding of the struggles that had been made and the sacrifices demanded of the workers in their efforts to emancipate themselves from wage-slavery. I knew the struggle must go on and I was determined to take an active part in it (Haywood 1966, 79).

In 1901, while living in Denver, Colorado, and working as Secretary-Treasurer of the WFM, Haywood and other officers of the Federation joined the Socialist Party. The principles of social-ism were formally adopted by a convention of the Federation, together with a resolution calling for a vigorous campaign of education among the membership. Eugene V. Debs took an active part in this campaign, which was carried on in conjunction with agitation for an eight-hour working day and improved conditions in mines and mills. Strikes were frequent, and they often led to confrontations between strikers and armed forces called out by governors at the instigation of mine and mill owners. In this "crucible of Colorado" as Haywood called it, tensions ran high; workers were imprisoned, deported, and some were slain. Haywood was tireless in these struggles, speaking at meetings of the unions, negotiating with representatives of the employers, governors, and judges, writing for newspapers and magazines, trading invective and blows with members of the "Citizens Alliance", self-appointed vigilantes of the rights of property. He was frequently jailed, bringing periods of relief to his wife who could then tell herself and the children that he was not likely to be shot while in the sheriff's custody.

The Western Federation of Miners was now strongly committed to industrial unionism. At its 1904 convention, plans were developed for the amalgamation of the entire working class into one general organization, and the executive board was instructed by the convention to carry out this program. Interest in industrial unionism was also developing in other parts of the country. A conference was to be held in Chicago on January 2, 1905. The letter of invitation, which went to about 30 people, contained the following paragraph:

> Asserting our confidence in the ability of the working class, if correctly organized in both political and industrial lines, to take possession of and operate successfully . . . the industries of the country; believing that working-class political expression, through the Socialist ballot, in order to be sound, must have its economic counterpart in a labor organization builded as the structure of socialist society, embracing within itself the working class in approximately the same groups and departments and industries that the workers would assume in the working-class administration of the Cooperative Commonwealth . . we invite you to meet us at Chicago, Monday, January second, 1905, in secret conference to discuss ways and means of uniting the working people of America in correct revolutionary principles, regardless of any general labor organization of past or present, and only restricted by such basic principles as will insure its integrity as a real protector of the interest of the workers (ibid. 175).

When the conference convened, Bill Haywood was elected chairman. It proceeded to draft and approve a manifesto which brought into being the Industrial Workers of the World (IWW, also known, more or less affectionately, as the Wobblies). It was signed by 27 delegates, among them Eugene V. Debs; Mother Jones, an organizer in the West Virginia coal mines; Charles H. Moyer, President of the Western Federation of Miners; and, of course, Haywood. The manifesto called for a convention to meet in Chicago in June, 1905. It evoked "the irrepressible conflict between the capitalist class and the working class" as well as "the possibility of establishing an industrial democracy, wherein there shall be no wage slavery, but where the workers will own the tools which they operate, and the product which they alone will enjoy" (ibid. 176).

On the back of the Manifesto the requirements for an industrial organization of the workers were listed. These were a summary of Haywood's own views on combining struggle for immediate and revolutionary goals: (1) It must combine the wage workers in such a way that it can most successfully fight the battles and protect the interests of the working people of today in their struggle for fewer hours, more wages and better conditions. (2) It must offer a final solution of the labor problem—an emancipation from strikes, injunctions and bullpens.

Then came this paragraph:

> Observe, also, how the growth and development of this organization will build up within itself the structure of an Industrial Democracy—a Workers' Cooperative Republic—which must finally burst the shell of capitalist government, and be the agency by which the working people will operate the industries and appropriate the products to themselves (ibid. 179).

The Chicago convention in June, 1905, brought together 200 delegates representing unions with some 300,000 members. This was the founding convention of the IWW. Haywood presided and was elected permanent chairman of the convention. In his opening speech Haywood stated:

> This is the Continental Congress of the working-class. We are here to confederate the workers of this country into a working-class movement that shall have for its purpose the emancipation of the working-class from the slave bondage of capitalism . . . The aims and objects of this organization shall be to put the working-class in possession of the economic power, the means of life, in control of the machinery of

production and distribution, without regard to capitalist masters. . . . There is not a man who has an ounce of honesty in his make-up but recognizes the fact that there is continuous struggle between the two classes, and this organization will be formed, based and founded on the class struggle, having in view no compromise and no surrender, and but one object and one purpose, and that is to bring the workers of this country into the possession of the full value of the product of their toil (ibid. 181–2).

In another speech at the convention Haywood dealt with the fact that the American Federation of Labor did not stand with the IWW on these big questions:

We recognize that this is a revolutionary movement and that the capitalists are not the only foes that you are to fight, but the most ardent enemy will be the pure and simple trade unionist. But there is only a few of him. He is not very well organized. You have got a tremendous field to work in. There are at least 20,000,000 unorganized workers in the United States of America, to say nothing of Canada. This industrial union movement is broad enough to take in all of them, and we are here for the purpose of launching that union that will open wide its doors to the working class . . . and just as surely as the sun rises, when you get the working class organized economically, it will find its proper reflection at the polls (ibid. 184–5).

In tsarist Russia, the red flag of revolution had been raised at Odessa in 1905. The new organization sent greetings to workers in struggle whose goals they shared. A longshoreman introduced such a resolution on Odessa, which ended:

Resolved, that we, the industrial unionists of America in convention assembled, urge our Russian fellow-workmen on in their struggle, and express our heartfelt sympathy with the victims of outrage, oppression and cruelty, and pledge our moral support and promise financial assistance as much as lies within our power, to our persecuted, struggling and suffering comrades in far-off Russia (ibid. 187).

Though Haywood was nominated to become president of the new organization and doubtless would have been elected, he declined with the explanation that he had just been re-elected Secretary-Treasurer of the Western Federation of Miners and wished not to leave that job. After Haywood had declined, Charles O. Sherman of the Metal and Machine Workers was elected presi-

dent. Haywood returned to the always turbulent industrial bat-
tlegrounds of the West feeling, he said, "that the Industrial Workers of the World had a great future before it" (ibid. 189).

On December 30, 1905, the former governor of Idaho, Frank
Steunenberg, was killed by a bomb at his home in Caldwell, Idaho.
The Idaho authorities seized the opportunity to arrest, charge and
prosecute the leading officers of the Western Federation of Miners
for murder. Colorado officials cooperated by allowing these residents of Denver, including Haywood, to be arrested and whisked
off to Idaho without warrants or extradition proceedings. After this
kidnapping, the defendants were kept in prison in Idaho for eight-
een months while the state tried to prepare a case against them.
Haywood used this unaccustomed leisure to study Shakespeare
and other classics of English literature, the writings of Marx and
Engels, and works of history, especially on the French Revolution.
He also took a correspondence course in law, though his experience with the law in Idaho and Colorado, he said, "made me
unwilling to become involved in a profession that was so crooked
and so meaningless for the working class" (ibid. 199).

Haywood was the first of the three defendants to be tried.
William E. Borah, recently elected United States Senator from
Idaho, led the state's team of lawyers as a special prosecutor.[2]
Clarence Darrow and Edmund H. Richardson acted as lawyers for
the defendants. Haywood wanted to have the Socialist leader,
Eugene V. Debs, present to report on the trial and make full use of
its political impact, but Darrow objected. Haywood suspected that
Darrow wanted to take no chances that someone other than he,
Darrow, should "be recognized as the most prominent person in
the trial". Darrow's superb skill as a defense attorney and swayer
of juries did not change Haywood's low opinion of the profession.
(There were a few lawyers whom he respected, among them
Richardson and John Murphy, who represented the WFM in
Denver.)

After the state had finished presenting its case, Haywood took the
stand in his own defense. He was examined and cross-examined
about the strong denunciations of then Governor Steunenberg by
Haywood and the Western Federation of Miners during some
Idaho miners' strikes:

Senator Borah: You felt very bitter against Governor Steunenberg.
Haywood: Yes, I felt toward him much as I did toward you and others
who were responsible for martial law and the bull-pen in the Coeur
d'Alenes (ibid. 213).

Eighty-seven witnesses from several of the Western states went
of their own accord, without subpoenas, to testify on Haywood's
behalf. The defense attorneys made good use of the fact that
Haywood had had no communication with Orchard (the prosecution's chief witness, who claimed he had placed the bomb on
Haywood's urging) for at least eight months prior to the fatal
explosion. Orchard himself was not charged, suggesting a dirty
deal with the prosecutors as a means of framing the defendants. In
the end, Haywood was acquitted following the jury's verdict of
"not guilty".

The trial brought national attention to Haywood and the Western Federation of Miners. Correspondents of many papers covered
it. The *New York American,* a Hearst paper, put out a special
edition carrying nothing except articles about the big case in
Boise, Idaho.

While Haywood and other defendants were being held in the
Idaho jail, Maxim Gorky visited New York from Russia. He sent
them a telegram of greetings from Russian workers. It is probable
that by this time (1906) Lenin had heard of Bill Haywood.

A Socialist Congress of the Second International meeting in
1907 in Stuttgart, Germany, with Lenin in attendance, sent Haywood the following message:

The International Congress sends William Haywood the congratula-
tions of the Socialist movement of the world in view of the magnificent
fight he put up in the interests of the organized workers of the United
States. It condemns emphatically the attempt of the mine owners to
have an innocent person punished by law only because of his services
to the cause of the organized workers. The Congress sees in the legal
proceedings and in the systematic campaign of slander carried on by
the entire capitalist press against Haywood the expression of the class
policy of the bourgeoisie of America, which is coming more and more to
the fore, and of the bourgeoisie's total lack of tolerance and sense of
honor in all occasions when its profits and its power are threatened.
The congress also congratulates the Socialists of the United States on
the enthusiasm and solidarity with which they resisted this attack. The

class conscious proletariat of Europe looks upon the enormous strength manifested by this act of solidarity as a guarantee of unity for the future and hopes that the American proletariat will show the same solidarity and determination in the fight for its complete emancipation (ibid. 220).

Haywood was naturally jubilant at victory in the Idaho court. A trial of another of the three defendants, George Pettibone, also ended in an acquittal. The state's prime witness, Orchard, was by then thoroughly discredited. Idaho moved to dismiss the charges against the third defendant, Charles H. Moyer, President of the Western Federation of Miners. Colorado gave up plans to prosecute Haywood and Moyer for other diabolical explosions also laid on them by Orchard. In Haywood's words,

> The mine owners were whipped in the Boise trial, and they knew they would be whipped again if ever they attempted to try any of us for these crimes, of which they themselves had indubitably been guilty (ibid. 222).

Since the trial had made him a celebrity, Haywood was much in demand from coast to coast as a speaker to groups which appreciated his revolutionary fervor. He campaigned hard for Debs for President in the 1908 election. He became a member of the National Executive Committee of the Socialist Party. When a massacre of gold miners occurred in the Lena River region of Siberia, Haywood introduced a resolution, approved by the Executive Committee, condemning the tsar and the British gold mining companies "for the murder of miners who had gone on strike to improve their working conditions."

In 1910, the Socialist Party sent him as a delegate to the Socialist Congress of the Second International held in Copenhagen. There he met Clara Zetkin and Alexandra Kollontai, who served as his interpreters at public meetings. Haywood was then more of an international celebrity with the general public than was the head of the Russian delegation. Lenin had to remind Haywood years later in Moscow that they had already met in Copenhagen. Haywood could not have known in 1910, of course, who among the many delegates at the Congress was destined to lead the first socialist revolution.

In Paris Haywood met William Z. Foster, who had attended an International Labor Congress in Budapest as a delegate of the IWW. Foster had formed a friendship with the French delegates and was absorbing some of their ideas on syndicalism. Haywood always insisted that there was a difference of theory between industrial unionism and syndicalism. The syndicalists wished to coordinate the different trades and crafts, whereas Haywood wanted to organize the whole working class along industrial lines. When Foster returned to the United States he wrote articles on revolutionary syndicalism for the IWW papers. Later he started the Syndicalist League with its own newspaper (ibid. 232).

When Haywood returned to the United States he threw himself into organizing for the IWW. He assisted Joseph Ettor and Elizabeth Gurley Flynn, two of the most successful IWW organizers on the East coast. Soon Haywood was called to Chicago to help organize the clothing workers, then to Pennsylvania to help in a strike of steel workers, then to Louisiana, Arkansas and Texas to confer with lumber workers. In Alexandria, Louisiana, he contributed to the merger of black and white workers of the Timber Workers Union into one convention. Until then they had been meeting in separate conventions, as Louisiana law required.

In 1911 and 1912 the textile workers of Lawrence, Massachusetts, went on strike to force employers to improve their pay and working conditions. Joseph Ettor and Haywood were asked by the strikers to give them assistance, so they were soon on the scene. The strike spread until about 25,000 workers were taking part. The entire textile industry of Lawrence and vicinity was "shut down tight". When Ettor was arrested and charged with murdering an Italian girl, Haywood became chairman of the strike committee (Ettor was ultimately acquitted). Again he was at the center of an important class struggle that concentrated the attention of millions. A writer for a conservative weekly, *Outlook,* gave a description of Haywood at this time which, despite the author's intention, pleased Haywood so much that he reproduced it in his autobiography:

> Haywood does not want unions of weavers, unions of spinners, unions of loom-fixers, unions of wool-sorters, but he wants one comprehensive union of all textile workers, which in time will take over the textile factories, as the steel workers will take over the steel mills and the railway workers the railways. Haywood interprets the class conflict literally as a war which is always on, which becomes daily more bitter and uncompromising, which can end only with the conquest of capi-

talistic society by proletarians or wage workers, organized industry by industry.

Haywood places no trust in trade agreements, which, according to his theory, lead merely to social peace and "put the workers to sleep." Let the employer lock out his men when he pleases, and let the workmen strike when they please. He is opposed to arbitration, conciliation, compromise; to sliding scales, profit sharing, welfare work; to everything, in short, which may weaken the revolutionary force of the workers. He does not ask for the closed shop or the official recognition of the union, for he has no intention of recognizing the employer. What he desires is not a treaty of industrial peace between the two high contracting parties, but merely the creation of a proletarian impulse which will eventually revolutionize society. Haywood is a man who believes in men, not as you and I believe in them, but fervently, uncompromisingly, with an obstinate faith in the universal goodwill and constancy of the workers worthy of a great religious leader. This is what makes him supremely dangerous (ibid. 248).

In this Massachusetts strike, as in so many others led by the IWW, Samuel Gompers of the American Federation of Labor withheld support and did what he could to force the strikers to surrender. Haywood came to regard Gompers as a worse enemy to the working class than the owners of the factories, because he was an enemy within their own class.

The strike ended with a sweeping victory for the workers. Wages were increased substantially and hours of labor reduced. Haywood considered the strike a magnificent demonstration of what solidarity can do for workers. Some 25 different nationalities were heavily represented among the textile workers. Haywood naturally and enthusiastically led them in singing the "International" at the victory celebration. He made the most of what had become a political event. Gompers stayed away.

In these class battles the factory owners made use of the stars and stripes to whip up patriotic opposition to the IWW. Gompers tried to be more patriotic than the owners and almost dressed himself in the flag. To Haywood this was treason to the working class, disguised as a mystical loyalty to country and an inherited flag. Either Gompers had been taken in as a simpleton or he was a deliberate traitor to his class. Haywood made no objection when red flags appeared among his strikers. To him they were a symbol of the future which he longed to help bring into being.

Strikes among silk workers at Paterson, New Jersey, among rubber workers at Akron, Ohio, among hop pickers in California, lumbermen in the Northwest and iron miners in Minnesota brought still more notoriety to Haywood and the IWW. Haywood was by now a marked man with aroused enemies who wielded wealth and power.

The outbreak of war in Europe caused the Second International to break up. Class solidarity gave way to national loyalties. Haywood, foreseeing U.S. entry into the war, was determined to save the IWW from such an ignominious fate. He promoted the following "Declaration", modeled on a Lenin–supported resolution at the Zimmerwald Conference and adopted by the IWW at its 1916 convention.

> We, the Industrial Workers of the World, in Convention assembled, hereby reaffirm our adherence to the principles of industrial unionism, and we dedicate ourselves to the unflinching, unfaltering prosecution of the struggle for the abolition of wage slavery, and the realization of our ideal in industrial democracy. With the European war for conquest and exploitation raging and destroying the lives, class consciousness and unity of the workers, and the ever-growing agitation for military preparedness clouding the main issues and delaying the realization of our ultimate aim with patriotic and, therefore, capitalistic aspirations, we openly declare ourselves the determined opponents of all nationalistic sectionalism, or patriotism, and the militarism preached and supported by our one enemy, the capitalist class. We condemn all wars, and for the prevention of such, we proclaim the anti-militarist propaganda in time of peace, thus promoting Class Solidarity among the workers of the entire world, and, in time of war, the General Strike in all industries. We extend assurances of both moral and material support to all the workers who suffer at the hands of the capitalist class for their adhesion to these principles and call on all workers to unite themselves with us, that the reign of the exploiters may cease and this earth be made fair through the establishment of the Industrial Democracy (ibid. 294–5).

With United States entry into the war, emergency measures were passed by several states and the federal government. These laws against "criminal syndicalism" were designed to destroy the IWW by making it a crime to be a member. In September, 1917, secret agents of the Department of Justice suddenly raided and occupied IWW offices all over the United States. On the basis of the thousands of documents seized, prosecutions were begun in California, Kansas and Illinois. Haywood was arrested, jailed and tried in a federal District Court in Chicago. Conviction was a foregone conclusion. Defendants' lawyers did what they could to turn the prosecution around and make the case a trial of the government, the social system and the war. Haywood was accused in the indictment of "conspiring". His attorney asked him if he was conspiring to prevent profiteering from war. Haywood replied:

> We are conspiring. We are conspiring to prevent the making of profits on labor power in any industry. We are conspiring against the dividend makers. We are conspiring against rent and interest. We want to establish a new society where people can live without profit, without dividends, without rent and without interest if it is possible; and it is possible, if people will live normally, live like human beings should live. I would say that if that is a conspiracy, we are conspiring (ibid. 322).

The jury found Haywood, along with 92 other defendants, guilty as charged. Judge Kenesaw M. Landis imposed heavy fines and prison sentences. Haywood was sentenced to serve twenty years in a federal penitentiary and fined $30,000. He entered the prison at Leavenworth, Kansas, in September, 1918.

An appeal was filed with the federal Circuit Court of Appeals. On July 28, 1919, Haywood was released from prison on bond pending the outcome of his appeal. With the war over, there was some hope that the Appellate Court would reverse the convictions. But when its decision came down, the prison sentences were affirmed, including that of Haywood. Only the fines were eliminated. Another appeal was taken to the Supreme Court, and Haywood continued free on bond. He was told there was little chance of a reversal. He faced the prospect of a return to Leavenworth with a twenty-year sentence. He wrote in his autobiography:

> I learned that President Harding was interviewed by Meyer London, Socialist Congressman from the State of New York, (who) was told by the President that the IWW members would be pardoned with the exception of Haywood, whom they were going to hold (ibid. 359).

While these appeals were pending the IWW received a lengthy letter from the Communist International. It outlined the points in common held by the IWW and the Communists. It analyzed the capitalist state and the role of the dictatorship of the proletariat. It told how the Soviet state of workers and peasants was constructed. The receipt of this letter Haywood called "a momentous circumstance in my somewhat eventful life". He exclaimed to Ralph Chaplin: "Here is what we have been dreaming about; here is the IWW all feathered out!" He was surely entitled to make the following boast:

> While it was addressed to the IWW as an organization, I felt, as I knew many other members did, that it was a tribute to ourselves, as each had helped to build this class conscious movement (ibid. 360).

The Communist Party of the United States, founded in 1919, was going through the travail of birth. Haywood joined in 1920. Among others of his co-workers who joined were William Z. Foster from the Syndicalist League (1921)[3] and a bit later, Elizabeth Gurley Flynn from the IWW (1926).

Friends were advising Haywood not to acquiesce in a return to prison. He agreed that the Soviet Republic could become his new base for a still useful life. He was 52 years old. In the spring of 1921 he obtained passage out of New York on a vessel bound for Latvia. In May he arrived in Moscow.

Sebald Rutgers

Sebald Justinus Rutgers was born in Leyden, Holland, in 1879, the son of a strong-willed physician who in mid-life had abandoned his theology and his pastorate to take up medicine as a calling he considered more useful to mankind. The family settled in Rotterdam, and the father built up a substantial practice. Young Sebald grew up in a household of books and comfort, where the works of Saint Simon, Fourier and Owen were admired and discussed. Sebald's father contributed a book of his own to utopian socialist literature, a volume entitled *The Year 2000*. The family's morality put a premium on the duty of study and achievement and on the higher duty of doing something useful for the human race.

Sebald responded positively to a formation of opportunity and challenge. At the age of 17 he entered the Polytechnical School (now the Technical University) in Delft, the Netherlands, and began the study of engineering. He was a brilliant student and graduated with distinction in 1900. His years as a student at the Polytechnical School also proved to be important in the development of his political commitment. He studied the writings of Marx and joined a circle of revolutionary-minded students who published their own magazine, *In de Nevel* (*In the Mist*). Sebald became a regular contributor, striving to deal with his topic in a Marxist way. After several summers of obligatory military training, he wrote a brochure entitled *Kazernetoestanden* (*Barracks Regimen*), summarizing his Marxist reflections on military conscription and training in a capitalist society. In 1899 Sebald joined the Social Democratic Workers Party. As this party evolved into a left and right wing, Rutgers was a part of the left. He stayed with this fraction when it broke off in 1907 to become the Social Democratic Party, a small Marxist party led by David Wynkoop. (This party would become the Communist Party of Holland in 1918 and later the Communist Party of the Netherlands.)

Rutgers began his career as a professional engineer in Rotterdam. Reinforced concrete was just then beginning to be employed as a construction material, and Rutgers saw its revolutionary potential for providing strength while reducing cost and weight. He submitted a design for a bridge to be constructed in Rotterdam using the new technique. It was selected, and amidst much skepticism among more conservative engineers it passed all tests and made Rutgers's reputation as an engineer. As a member of the Construction Department of Rotterdam he designed a fast and economical way to rebuild the city's harbor. In 1908 he was named head of the department of construction and hydraulic engineering of the Royal Netherlands Institute of Engineers. He represented the Netherlands in international congresses on reinforced concrete as an Assistant Professor at Delft. His professional articles appeared in the Dutch magazine, *Engineers*. His name became known abroad, and he was invited to collaborate in the reconstruction of the harbor of Valparaiso, Chile.

Despite this success and renown, Rutgers made it his guiding precept not to shut himself up in his profession. He took an active part in the work of his party. As a member of the party's commission on living conditions of workers he moved about in working class districts, chatting and observing, making time to learn about a reality of hardship till then unknown to him.

He had an ability to get things done, and he used it in his party work. Longshoremen were being exploited by agents and bar owners who combined to make the long and uncertain periods of waiting for jobs costly to the longshoremen and profitable to the bars. Rutgers promoted the construction of a hiring hall, the first in Rotterdam, and with it gained much honor and gratitude from the longshoremen. He also played an important part in planning, financing and building a workers' cooperative equipped with food store, bakery, printing shop and meeting room. He was publicly congratulated by party leaders at the opening ceremony for his role in the creation of a "fortress of the working class".

Notwithstanding this drive for work and achievement, Rutgers seemed most remarkable for his modesty, his good nature, his simple humanity which made it easy for him to relate to people of all types. His gifts and his experience combined to develop in him an inspiring confidence in what the future would bring. He had a contagious optimism.

Despite his politics and some criticism in his father's circle, Rutgers felt no need to break with his family's class. In the home of another elderly physician where Rutgers was frequently a guest, the audacity of his views and his easy optimism won the heart of the physician's daughter. She was soon accompanying him in street demonstrations and party work. Rutgers and Bartha Mees were married in 1902. She bore him three children and enjoyed with him a lifetime of foreign adventures and Communist party work, rounded out with final years in the stable comfort of a family home in the Netherlands.

In 1910 the desire to know more about a larger world than the Netherlands stirred Rutgers to make a move with his family to Sumatra in the East Indies. There Dutch was the language of the business and professional world and there his membership in the Royal Netherlands Institute of Engineers gave him a license to earn his living as an engineer. He established his own consulting office and had no trouble gaining clients. He was close to the colonial administration of the island and frequently in its employ. Here the contradiction between his own privileged status and his Marxist condemnation of the prevailing exploitation of the underlying population troubled him. As in the Netherlands, he was two people, and determined to develop both sides of his identity and destiny without sacrificing one to the other. While in Sumatra he maintained his membership in the Social Democratic Party and continued to contribute articles to its leftist newspaper, the *Tribune*. He spent nights preparing materials for two books, *Indonesia* and *The Peasant Question*, with which he hoped to advance his reputation as a Marxist thinker.

When war broke out in Europe in August, 1914, Rutgers knew the existing states would be shaken to their foundations. He thought the war could not last long, and he wanted to return to the Netherlands as soon as possible, foreseeing a period of political crisis and revolutionary opportunity. He wound up his professional commitments in Sumatra and with his family departed in March, 1915, via China, Japan and the United States. By the time they arrived in New York three months later, the prospects for a quick end to the war had dimmed. Rutgers decided he and his family should stay in New York for an indefinite period while watching the development of events in Europe. He was able to have himself named purchasing agent for several Dutch East Indies companies that needed to find American sources of equipment and supply to substitute for those European sources disrupted by the war. Again Rutgers made the most of his talents and training in order to provide a comfortable home for himself and family, this time at Manhattan Beach in Brooklyn. He soon found himself in great demand by Dutch and Indonesian banks and industries, with whom he did business involving millions of dollars and important technical projects. This work gave him the occasion to improve his command of English and his knowledge of American production techniques.

It would have been easy to give himself entirely to this much appreciated and well rewarded employment in the service of the Dutch bourgeoisie. Rutgers's character was not formed under hardship. His trials rather took the form of glittering temptations. And once again he kept a part of himself for another destiny. He joined the Socialist Party and became a member of its left wing. He helped organize the League of Socialist Propaganda in America, with headquarters in Boston, Massachusetts, and in this enterprise made contact with many of the leading activists in the American socialist movement. The League issued a strongly leftist "Appeal" the text of which reached Lenin who was then living in Switzerland. It stressed the importance of struggle against the opportunism of the Second International and called for the creation of a

Third International with revolutionary goals. Lenin replied to it with enthusiasm, beginning a relationship between him and Rutgers that became important to both over the next few years.

A publication closely identified with the Industrial Workers of the World entitled *International Socialist Review* opened its pages to both Lenin and Rutgers. The militant opposition of the IWW to the war, its support of the call by the Zimmerwald Conference for international proletarian unity and its demonstrated ability to lead strikes by masses of workers in the United States won the respect of both Lenin and Rutgers, and both were pleased to reach an IWW audience through the pages of the *International Socialist Review*. This coming together in 1915–1916 of Lenin, Rutgers and the IWW (in which Bill Haywood was playing a leading role) laid a groundwork of acquaintance and collaboration which was later to become a key factor in the development of our story.

The October Revolution in 1917 in Russia and the installation of a government headed by Lenin and the Bolsheviks immediately struck Rutgers as an event of enormous importance in world history. As the American press intensified its denunciation of the Bolsheviks, Rutgers took a stand in the League of Socialist Propaganda and in the Socialist Party with those who hailed the new regime. He also decided to bring his own life to fruition by dedicating it fully to the building of socialist production in the Soviet Republic. He had training, experience and firm political convictions which included a belief in the importance of internationalism, in the duty and responsibility of socialist revolutionaries to aid each other across national frontiers. He knew that the socialist regime in the Soviet Republic was engaged in a life-and-death struggle and that industrial reconstruction and expansion was one of its crucial challenges. He was sure it could make good use of a dedicated Dutch engineer. The attraction of this theater of struggle overcame any desire in Rutgers to return to the Netherlands or stay longer in the United States.

His wife, Bartha, shared his excitement, so they made plans to close up their home in Manhattan Beach and seek entry into the Soviet Republic. Because the war was still going on in Europe, they elected to make their approach from the Far East. In May, 1918, they departed from New York traveling west across the United States and thence across the Pacific to Japan. There they separated from their children, ages eight, ten and twelve, who remained in Japan in the care of friends.

Rutgers established contact with Japanese socialists and disclosed his plans to enter the Soviet Republic. When he and Bartha departed from Japan for Vladivostok in August, 1918, Rutgers carried with him a resolution of solidarity addressed to the Bolsheviks from Japanese socialists. This document he had to keep carefully hidden during the journey across Siberia and Eastern Russia, which were then theaters of civil war. Rutgers was traveling as a Dutch citizen, a member of the Royal Netherlands Institute of Engineers and advisor to the Netherlands East Indies Railroad Company, giving as the reason for his entry a desire to seek business opportunities for his clients. This explanation, added to their bourgeois appearance and manners, enabled him and his wife to cross three fronts, passing the scrutiny of innumerable officials who were seeking to intercept and arrest any friends of the Bolsheviks. They arrived in Moscow on September 23, 1918, and were assigned a room in the Metropol Hotel.

Rutgers delivered to *Pravda* the declaration of solidarity from Japanese socialists. This brought an invitation to meet with the Foreign Minister, Chicherin, followed by a meeting with Sverdlov, President of the All-Russian Central Executive Committee. Sverdlov, learning of Rutgers's experience and desire to work in the Soviet Republic, sent him to Pavlovich, head of construction projects. Soon Rutgers was advised that he had been named general inspector of waterways. He was also invited by Sverdlov to make a report on "the situation abroad" before members of the Central Executive Committee. Rutgers knew a great deal about reactions to the Bolshevik Revolution in the Netherlands, the United States and Japan. This was of great interest in Moscow. Lenin, however, was recovering from an attempt on his life and did not attend the Central Executive Committee meeting.

Some days later Rutgers received a message that he had an appointment to meet with Lenin in his office. Lenin was eager to listen to all that Rutgers could tell him about the attitude of different groups abroad toward the Bolsheviks. Lenin attached enormous importance to the possibility of revolutionary initiatives in Western Europe as an outcome of the terrible sufferings of the European peoples in the war just then coming to an end. The creation of a Third International with a revolutionary program was on Lenin's agenda. He found in Rutgers a proven and steadfast advocate of such a step. (Recall the 1915 Appeal of the League of Socialist Propaganda.) Rutgers was able to take part in the planning of the First Congress of the Third (Communist) International, which was held in Moscow in March, 1919. Rutgers attended as a delegate of the Communist Party of Holland and also of the left opposition in the Socialist Party of the United States. He undoubtedly earned the right to be named among the founders of the Third International.

During these first few months in Moscow, Rutgers was also commencing his work as an engineer. He studied the many unfinished hydro construction projects left over from tsarist times. With an interpreter he inspected port facilities in Petrograd, then traveled via the Neva River to Ladoga and Onega Lakes, then to Novgorod and via canals to the Volga River, visiting ports as far east as Kazan. He presented a report to the government with recommendations concerning restoration, repairs and new construction. Through his own eyes he was learning about the devastated condition of the nation's physical plant. The blockade by European powers was in effect. Everywhere he traveled he saw evidence of hunger, cold, disease and death.

In January, 1919, Rutgers began work in Latvia (where a Soviet Republic had been established a month earlier) on improving the port of Riga. Here many people spoke German, so Rutgers was relieved of some of his handicap of not knowing Russian or Latvian. In this project Rutgers could draw on his lengthy studies of reinforced concrete and his years of work on the port facilities of Rotterdam. He quickly established himself as an authority in his field and a valuable collaborator in the tasks of socialist construction.

The opportunities for work in a cause he cherished were stimulating. To those drains on his energy was added his work in preparing and participating in the First Congress of the Communist International. A few days after it closed, Rutgers was stricken with acute pneumonia. For two weeks he lay unconscious in his hotel room in Moscow. There were no supplies of oxygen and little in the way of medicine. Death could easily have been the outcome, and in fact news reached the Netherlands that he had died. Somehow he pulled through this ordeal, though he had to spend six months of convalescence in a sanatorium and was unable to return to work in Riga (where the new Latvian Soviet Republic was destined soon to be overthrown).

Plans for establishment of a Western Bureau of the Third International in Europe were being discussed during the summer of 1919. The availability of Rutgers to undertake a leading role once his health permitted was a decisive factor in choice of the Netherlands as a headquarters. Rutgers had conferences with Lenin and others in Moscow who were promoting the new International as to what should be undertaken by the Western Bureau. When Rutgers departed in October, 1919, he carried with him a letter of greeting to all friends in Western Europe, penned and signed by Lenin. A second Congress of the International was to meet in 1920, and it was Rutger's responsibility to promote attendance and support by leading radicals of the European countries and the United States. Lenin gave him names of persons he considered to be the most promising participants from various Western countries. Through these contacts Rutgers became well known among European socialists as an emissary of Lenin.

Rutgers arrived in the Netherlands after an absence of nearly a decade. He was still weak from his pneumonia and was also suffering from diabetes. His doctor ordered complete rest, but Rutgers simply could not lay aside the responsibility he had assumed. He took on the job as General Secretary of the Western Bureau, established in Amsterdam and therefore known in history as the Amsterdam Bureau. Other members were Herman Gorter, Anton Pannekoek, David Wynkoop, Henriette Roland-Holst and Willem Van Ravesteyn.

Wynkoop had emerged as the principal leader of the newly formed Communist Party of Holland. He was too absorbed in the work of his own Party to give much of his time to the problems of the Amsterdam Bureau. Gorter and Pannekoek had serious differences with Wynkoop, and they used the new Bureau to publicize their views. The poet, Roland-Holst, and the historian, Van Ravestyn, the latter with some reservations, acquiesced in the Gorter-Pannekoek line without fully understanding its sectarian character. Rutgers, too, though he was closer to agreement with Wynkoop on these basic questions, allowed the *Bulletin of the Provisional Bureau in Amsterdam of the Communist Interna-*

tional to be used to publish the theses of Gorter and Pannekoek as theses of the Dutch Left, which apparently included Rutgers, the General Secretary of the Bureau, as well as Wynkoop and the other Bureau members.

These Dutch pamphlets advocated abstention from participation in bourgeois parliaments; they rejected policies of maneuvering and compromise with bourgeois parties; and they declaimed against participation by Communists in reformist labor unions. These theses were ratified by an international conference of delegates recruited by Rutgers and held in the Netherlands under the auspices of the Amsterdam Bureau. Among those attending were Clara Zetkin from Germany, Sylvia Pankhurst from England and Louis Fraina from the United States.

Lenin saw in such theses further evidence of a dangerous sectarian leftism among many leaders of the socialist movements of Europe. In April, 1920, he took up his pen to attack "left-wing communism" as manifested in Germany, England, the Netherlands and Italy. Though Rutgers was not mentioned by name (as were numerous others), the Bulletin of the Amsterdam Bureau was quoted and severely criticized. Lenin's pamphlet was a powerful polemic that came to be accepted in the Communist International as a correct analysis of the problem and a justified identification and condemnation of sectarian leftism as an "infantile disorder". It was ascribed to immaturity and lack of experience. Like measles and chicken pox, it was not likely to prove permanently disabling, and it was widespread among even the healthiest of revolutionaries in their early years of dedicated struggle.

Rutgers described this painful episode as "a decisive lesson which I tried to assimilate" (Trincher, 1967, 85). Wynkoop disclaimed all responsibility and wrote to Lenin protesting against attribution of the Bureau's Bulletins to the Dutch Communist Party. Lenin corrected his text in later editions to read "some members of the Communist Party of Holland". Rutgers joined Wynkoop in an endorsement of Lenin's critique. Gorter and Pannekoek did not repent. The Amsterdam Bureau was in discredit at the Second Congress of the Comintern, held in Moscow in July and August, 1920. Wynkoop headed the Dutch delegation and probably aided in the repair of Rutgers's damaged reputation. In Bolshevik circles Rutgers, still admired and respected, was now perceived as prone to leftist errors. This was no great handicap, however, since he had acknowledged his mistake, and Lenin himself described an ability to learn from one's mistakes, inevitable in such a struggle, as the virtue of a true Communist.

Rutgers was unable to attend the Second Congress for reasons of health. His doctor in the Netherlands, worried by the lingering effects of his illnesses, prescribed a winter in Italy. Accompanied by Bartha and their youngest child, Gertrude, and by a Dutch writer, Augusta de Wit, Rutgers traveled to the region around La Spezia on the Ligurian Sea. There they rented a villa at Lerici, and Rutgers began a routine of rest and study. He was determined to return to the Soviet Republic as soon as his health permitted.

To correct the language deficiency that had burdened his earlier work in 1918 and 1919, he decided to undertake the study of Russian in his now abundant spare time. Augusta de Wit had a suggestion for solving the problem of finding a tutor. In a sanatorium in Davos, Switzerland, she had met Bronka Kornblitt, a Polish Communist who had worked as an underground revolutionary in tsarist Russia. A victim of tuberculosis, she had undergone an operation which left her with one lung but an undaunted will to live and work. Rutgers wrote her an invitation to join them at Lerici and teach him Russian. To his great good fortune, he also acquired in Bronka a self-sacrificing secretary and a devoted helper in projects still to come. She becomes a character in our story.

The routine at Lerici gave Rutgers a chance to review the many observations he had made in Siberia and Russia and to think through the problem of assisting the Soviet Republic with technology from the more advanced countries. He wrote out a plan for creating a model industry with the help of foreign workers. We will explore this document in the next chapter. Bronka typed it for him with growing enthusiasm. She was sure there would be a role for her in such an enterprise.

Suddenly the Italian police decided the presence of the Rutgers family was an offense and a menace no longer to be tolerated. Rutgers, Bartha and daughter Gertrude were arrested and taken to La Spezia for questioning. Orders came from Rome that they were to be deported. By train they were taken to the Austrian border and released for travel to Vienna. There Austrian Communists (especially Hans Wertheim) gave them help in getting to

Berlin. Rutgers had decided to return to Moscow. Bartha would return to the Netherlands with Gertrude to await developments. These plans were communicated to Bronka and de Wit, who had remained behind in Italy under house arrest. Now a telegram arrived from Bronka. They were free to leave, and Bronka requested Rutgers to arrange her visa to Moscow. She too was restored and stirred by Rutgers's vision of the Soviet challenge. Rutgers was happy to comply.

Herbert S. Calvert

Herbert Stanley Calvert was born in California in 1889. If, as he believed, the blood of one of the principal founding families of the colonial province of Maryland flowed in his veins, it did not carry with it any inheritance of property and wealth. Throughout his childhood and youth his parents moved from place to place in a struggle to raise their fortunes above a level that bordered on poverty. When Herbert was about four years of age they moved to the farming country around Vincennes, Indiana, on the Wabash River. As they shifted from one small Indiana town to another over the next few years, Herbert was attending public schools and gaining confidence from the repeated experience of finding himself in a new situation. One of his teachers, who had become a superintendent of schools, was impressed with the young man's poise and intelligence and arranged for him to attend the Illinois State Normal University as a scholarship student. Herbert made good grades in his first year and might have stayed on to become a teacher in a midwestern school system had not another move of his family once again carried him to a new scene and new experiences. This time they migrated to the Pecos River valley in New Mexico.

Herbert for a while worked as a farm laborer, building irrigation reservoirs and learning to handle the four-mule teams that pulled gang plows, earth scoops and levelers. He and his father rented some land and tried to earn a living raising alfalfa. After the first crop had been cut, prospects looked so unpromising that Herbert decided to join his brother who had a job as a laborer on the Santa Fe Railroad. For seven years Herbert sold his labor to the railroad, usually as a bridge carpenter. He was learning skills, and he was beginning to supplement his growing class consciousness with a study of socialism. With his knowledge of the world of railroads, he traveled frequently, hobo-style, on freight trains in an ever-changing company of embittered men who were ready to listen to his judgments on the capitalist system. He impressed all by his fluency with words.

He tried to make a different life for himself as a salesman. A hardware company in Albuquerque, New Mexico, gave him a territory on a Navajo Indian reservation where he was to sell their wares on commission. He learned the Navajo tongue and cultivated the arts of salesmanship. They came naturally to him, and he soon decided to change his base to Los Angeles, already a thriving metropolis with a population of one million. There he continued to support himself as a traveling salesman of sewing machines and devoted his spare time to the study and promotion of socialism.

He joined the Socialist Party and became a follower of Eugene Debs. In this political circle he met Mellie Miller, daughter of a real estate entrepreneur who was a generous financial contributor to socialist causes. Mellie and Herbert married, with the blessing of her father. Mellie Calvert described the man she married as thin, intense, enthusiastic, concentrated, fiery, dramatic and colorful. In her more sober opinion he seemed too easily carried away by the force of his own rhetoric. He did love to talk.

Together he and Mellie helped create the Young People's Socialist League of Los Angeles. With dances and low-cost meals on Saturday nights the League successfully recruited young people and soon reached a membership of 1,500. Herbert and Mellie worked as volunteers in the office of Job Harriman, a socialist candidate for mayor of Los Angeles. They also helped to recruit some 1,000 families for a socialist colony established at Llano de Rio near Los Angeles.

When the first world war broke out in Europe, resistance to entry into the war by the United States became a lively political issue. In California and the Southwest this resistance frequently took the form of migration to Mexico. Colonies of Americans formed, strong in anti-war convictions and critical of the capitalist system. Calvert and his wife joined in this concentration of approximately ten thousand Americans in Mexico. He saw it as an opportunity to win new recruits to socialism. To earn a living the

Calverts invested their savings in the production of tomatoes for the California market. By utilizing a new technique with dust mulch (Calvert had seen it being used by truck farmers in California), productivity was raised sufficiently to make theirs a promising enterprise. This rosy prospect of rising income was outweighed in importance by other developments that occurred during their years in Mexico.

(The following account is based on an unpublished manuscript of Mellie Calvert and on a taped autobiographical account made by Herbert Calvert in 1971.)

It was during this period that they "met their first Bolsheviks." These contacts and discussions deepened Herbert's commitment and prepared him for what both he and his wife characterized as a decisive event in his life. This was the arrival in Mexico of copies of Lenin's *Letter to American Workers*, written in August, 1918. It had been published in New York in English in December, 1918. In it Lenin explained and justified the policies of the new government he headed. He laid great stress on the importance of international working-class support for the new "Republic of Soviets":

> We are now, as it were, in a besieged fortress, waiting for the other detachments of the world socialist revolution to come to our relief. These detachments *exist*, they are *more numerous* than ours, they are maturing, growing, gaining more strength the longer the brutalities of imperialism continue.

Just at that time, Lenin wrote, "the American revolutionary workers have to play an exceptionally important role as uncompromising enemies of American imperialism." He expressed the conviction that "we are invincible, because the world proletarian revolution is invincible."

It is clear from Lenin's letter that what he hoped for in the way of "support" was an adoption of "Communist, Bolshevik tactics" by the workers' movements in other countries, so that they too would march "towards the proletarian revolution, which alone is capable of saving dying culture and dying mankind." Lenin realistically acknowledged that the timing of such further revolutions was uncertain:

> We know that help from you will probably not come soon, comrade American workers, for the revolution is developing in different countries in different forms and at different tempos (and it cannot be otherwise). We know that although the European proletarian revolu-

tion has been maturing very rapidly lately, it may, after all, not flare up within the next few weeks. We are banking on the inevitability of the world revolution, but this does not mean that we are such fools as to bank on the revolution inevitably coming on a *definite* and early date.[4]

This letter of Lenin's contained no specific suggestion that American workers move with their skills and experience to the Soviet Republic and there assist in building up the shattered economy of the new workers' state. Nevertheless Calvert read such a call between the lines, and in time Calvert's free leap to this new idea would be justified by Lenin's own support of it. Lenin was virtually present at the conception: Calvert claimed, with confirmation from his wife, to have received an impulse from the Lenin letter that ultimately carried him to Moscow and to the creation of an American industrial colony in Siberia. When he first read the letter, he declared to Mellie, "I gotta answer that", his always unruly hair waving more wildly than usual. Mellie's reply was, "The hardships here in Mexico are bad enough."

The stimulation received from reading Lenin's words and from other reports on the Bolshevik Revolution produced in Calvert a desire to join the most maligned and the most notorious of the workers' organizations on the American scene as World War I came to a close. That was the Industrial Workers of the World, the Wobblies, so closely linked to the name of Bill Haywood. Calvert became a member of the IWW at the time of its worldwide notoriety and persecution as a revolutionary organization in the period 1918 to 1920. Lenin had hailed the IWW as a revolutionary proletarian movement with which the Bolsheviks had much in common.

Calvert chose Detroit as the best place for his entry, or reentry, into the American working class. He got a job in the heavy press forging department of the Ford automobile plant in a Detroit suburb, Highland Park. He was greatly impressed by the organization and efficiency of the Ford plant, and he strove to learn as much about it as he could. In his spare time he studied metallurgy and the operation of blast furnaces. His enthusiasm and abilities soon made him stand out, and he was promoted to a post as unit foreman. He was developing that reverence for machine industry which caused Tom Barker, a British colleague who met Calvert in 1921, to write of him as follows:

He sees the race of man with these mighty tools in his hands, throwing itself like a disciplined, singing army upon the earth and conquering her at last. . . . He is a poet of power, of real things, of forces and control (*British Labour Monthly*, London, 1970).

He also threw himself into recruiting for the IWW and mastering its doctrine. Its emphasis on the capability of blue collar workers to manage their factories without guidance from the absentee capitalists complemented and fortified his daily life experience as a competent worker and foreman.

He liked to emphasize that workers' control meant taking the fetters off production. With this special focus he became the initiator of an imaginative project to give the workers at Ford control of their plant for a month. Calvert learned during a Christmas holiday shutdown that the plant was not to reopen in January, 1921. He and four other workers thereupon drafted and distributed 5,000 copies of a leaflet entitled "From the Ford Men to the Ford Motor Company". It stated that, since the plant was to remain closed for at least a month, the regular Ford employees requested the use of the Ford plant during the month of January to make automobiles for themselves and family, one car per employee. "We will pay for all the raw materials used and return the plant in better condition than we receive it." The leaflet went on to say that all who wanted to work on such conditions should show up at the plant gate with their lunch pails, ready for work. This plan made eminent good sense to workers, most of whom could not afford to buy an automobile. On the appointed day 25,000 workers showed up in their work clothes. Management treated the proposal with scorn, and nothing more came of it. There had been no preparation to convert the proposal into a demand and a platform for struggle. Calvert was pleased at the impressive turnout of workers, in which he found proof of his ability to innovate with ideas.

The independence of trade unions from government control was an IWW first principle. Its syndicalism merged with a penchant for anarchism. In the Soviet Republic this doctrine was under attack in debates over the relationship between the Communist Party (Bolshevik) and the trade unions. That was an internal controversy about which Calvert had very little information. It was later to become a point of friction between Bolsheviks and the new leaders of the IWW. Dual unionism, supported in practice by the IWW, created another potential area of controversy. The IWW urged its members to stay out of the established unions of the labor movement (especially the American Federation of Labor) and to create their own more militant unions on industrial lines. Lenin, on the other hand, was urging revolutionaries in the capitalist countries to join and work in "reactionary" trade unions, where the mass of organized workers could be reached and influenced. (*Left-Wing Communism, an Infantile Disorder*, 1920).

It is not likely that Calvert had any clearly formed views on these lurking contradictions between Bolshevism and IWW doctrine. In 1920 he was enthusiastic about both. He worked hard to win the confidence of his IWW "fellow workers" (the required salute they used as a distinguishing password in referring to each other). And he watched for an opportunity to visit the Republic of Lenin. The invitation to the national leadership of the IWW to send delegates to an "International Congress of Red Trade Unions" to be held in Moscow in the spring of 1921 created the occasion he had been waiting for. The Detroit local of the Metal and Machinery Workers Industrial Union (IWW) rewarded Calvert by acting favorably on his request to be named a delegate to the Congress. Calvert judged *that* nomination to be a sufficient credential. The national office might not have agreed, so Calvert bought his own ticket to Windsor, Ontario, and to Montreal. There in February, 1921, he boarded a boat for Latvia. He used a passport borrowed from a Russian immigrant.

On board were some of the thousands of Russians, Finns, Latvians and other peoples of the tsarist empire who were now jubilantly returning to their native lands following years of exile in the United States and Canada. Calvert discussed with them how their skills, acquired by work in an advanced industrial system, could now best be utilized by the new Soviet Republic. To Calvert, it was imperative at this moment of history to show the world that workers have a supreme ability to organize and expand production. His theme evoked strong resonance in the returning migrants. It was an invigorating voyage toward a new future of unbounded promise. It added to Calvert's enthusiasm for some form of international effort by advanced workers to take part in the building of a productive economy in the Soviet Republic.

The last part of the journey, after disembarking in Libau, was made in a cold boxcar, unfurnished with either straw or paper. He was more than glad finally to find himself in Moscow.

2

NEGOTIATING AN AGREEMENT

Extreme diseases justify, nay demand, extreme remedies. The year 1921 was a year of terrible famine in the Soviet Republic. The extremity of the case helps us to understand the extremity of the measures approved by the Soviet government and the readiness of leading Communists in the Soviet Republic to invest hope and scarce resources in an unprecedented enterprise conceived and promoted by foreigners, most of whom had no experience in the peculiar reality of Russian conditions. For the creation of Kuzbas, an extraordinary degree of enthusiasm and determination was required of its founders. That was forthcoming. But it would have been fruitless without Soviet governmental approval and support; and undoubtedly that approval sprang from the desperate state of the Soviet economy. Decisions in 1921 were heavily influenced by the accumulated consequences of war, foreign interventions, blockade, drought and finally famine.

Russia had already been at war for three years when the October, 1917, revolution brought the Soviet Government to power. Within weeks military campaigns had been organized and launched against the new regime. In the ensuing war, which lasted another three years, Soviet forces had to be mobilized to fight on four major fronts. In Siberia Admiral Kolchak, with support from the United States and Japan, established a reactionary dictatorship at Omsk and began a military drive to the west. His armies penetrated almost to the Volga River before they were turned back by the Red

Army in the summer of 1919. In the south, General Denikin pushed northward from the Caucasus and gained control of Russia's granary, the Ukraine. His troops captured Kiev, Kursk, Kharkov and Orel. Another tsarist general, Yudenitch, headed a drive in the Baltic region against Petrograd from the west. After enormous damage to crops, farming equipment and factories and with heavy casualties, government forces finally turned back these attacks as well.

Besides giving military and financial aid to these sundry anti-Soviet armies, foreign governments further harrassed the new regime with direct interventions by their own armed forces. Thus an international or "inter-allied" force made up mostly of American and Japanese troops seized Vladivostok in the Far East while British and American troops predominated in the expeditionary army that occupied Archangel in the extreme north.

Then in 1920 Poland, with support from France, attacked the Ukraine. The Poles had captured Kiev and occupied parts of the western Ukraine before Soviet forces could mobilize a counter-offensive. When this came, it pushed the battle lines back into Poland and led to an armistice and negotiations. Peace was signed at Riga in March, 1921.

General Wrangel had succeeded Denikin in command of the anti-Soviet forces in the south. He continued to occupy the Crimean peninsula. Release of troops from the Polish front enabled the government finally to annihilate Wrangel in November, 1920.

Vast regions had been devastated in these battles. Among them were the Donets coal basin, which was left a ruin by the Denikin and Wrangel campaigns. This generated a shortage of coal severely affecting transport and manufacture. Textile and metal factories in Moscow and Petrograd required cotton from Turkestan and coal and iron from the Urals and the Donets. These sources of supply were cut off during the civil war, while a blockade enforced by Britain, France and the United States prevented imports of supplies from foreign sources.

Military campaigns in the agricultural regions completely disrupted the supply of food to city areas. Draft animals and cattle were spoils of war. Fields were cut up with trenches and barbed wire. Farm machinery was destroyed, buildings razed, water tanks and bridges burned or damaged.

These blows to the country's productive capacity would require skilled workers in a formidable labor of repair. But the life and death crises of the civil war had drawn the best workmen from their benches and placed them in command of Red Army military units. These advanced and spirited leaders of the proletariat, who knew what they were fighting for, were indispensable on the battle fronts. Casualties among them were high, the dearest cost of military victory over the counterrevolutionaries. Their loss to industry was keenly felt during the long period of civil war and for years after.[5]

Added to these trials were the effects of the blockade. Russian industry had always depended upon foreign countries for many articles which it could not itself manufacture. For example, there was no Russian manufacture of wire cable, which was essential to coal mining. As hoisting cables wore out, mines were compelled to shut down because the blockade denied access to foreign sources of supply. When a mine closed down, factories had to curtail production for lack of fuel. Locomotives and power stations stood idle because seamless tubing could not be imported for repair of boilers. As belts wore out on machinery, they could not be replaced, since they, too, were imported items. For lack of light bulbs many factories had to shut down in the early afternoon as daylight failed.

The blockade also stopped the importation of drugs and medicines. As a consequence, outbreaks of typhus, dysentery and cholera could not be controlled. The ravages of these epidemics spread throughout the land, causing thousands of deaths and further disruption of efforts to restore economic life. The blockade continued in effect until 1920 when negotiations to resume trade began. These finally led to a Russo–British Trade Agreement in March, 1921.

These many and varied scourges of the Russian people lowered their ability to deal with a severe drought that hit the land in 1920. This in turn produced famine conditions in 1921, particularly in the Volga region.

Thus the year 1921 was a year that challenged the initiative and resourcefulness of all friends of the new Soviet Republic. It had overcome obstacles on military and diplomatic fronts probably as great as any nation had ever known. Despite the intervention of 14 capitalist states and their ruthless blockade, the civil wars led by

Whiteguard generals financed from abroad had been put down and peace restored. It was a year of appalling hardship, hunger, disorganization and disease. But it was also a year to be remembered as an inspiring and animating time, because it brought a conviction of survival through hard-earned victories over dangerous and deadly enemies. Workers in foreign countries had contributed to those victories. The very desperation in economic conditions opened minds to innovation, enthusiasm from abroad and fresh historic initiatives.

Calvert arrived in Moscow in March, 1921. With other foreign delegates to the "Red Trade Union International" (formally, the Red International of Labor Unions, RILU), he was lodged in the Hotel Lux. This militant, internationalist workingclass setting was an ideal environment for the gestation of his notion that foreign workers should take part in the construction of industry in the new Soviet Republic. The need for help was brought home to him by his visits to the factories and workshops of Moscow. He wore out a pair of shoes on these tours, comparing what he saw with what he had experienced in the Ford plants of Detroit. He could see that the task confronting the revolutionary leaders to develop industrial production in this vast, backward and devastated country was urgent and enormous. Doubtless the very fate of the first socialist revolution hung in the balance.

There was a great deal of talk about Lenin's New Economic Policy, which was aimed primarily at strengthening the alliance of the revolutionary workers and the peasantry. NEP included a limited, temporary role for capitalist elements, including foreign capitalists, under the control of the Bolshevik state.

In a report delivered at the Tenth Congress of the Russian Communist Party (Bolshevik) on March 8, 1921, Lenin discussed the desperate situation: (*Collected Works*, 32: 181–2).

On November 23, (1920) the decree of the Council of People's Commissars was issued which dealt with the question of concessions in a form most acceptable to foreign capitalists. . . On the whole, it did not give rise to disagreements, although we heard not a few protests from workers and peasants. . . At all events, with this decree we have taken a step towards the establishment of concession relations. It must be said that actually—and this must never be forgotten—we have not succeeded in placing a single concession. There is a dispute among us about whether we should try to place concessions at all costs. Whether we succeed in doing so or not will not be decided by our disputes and decisions, but by international capital. . . . . The majority of the Central Committee, and I personally, adopted the point of view that these concessions are necessary, and we shall ask you to support this point of view with your authority. This union with the state trusts of the advanced countries is absolutely essential for us owing to the fact that our economic crisis is so profound that we shall be unable to restore our ruined economy by our own efforts, without equipment and technical assistance from abroad. . . . No one who contemplates our present position at all soberly can have any doubt whatever that without this we shall find ourselves in a very difficult position, and that we shall never catch up with them without the tremendous exertion of all our efforts . . . of course, we shall have to pay a heavy price for this thing, but we have no alternative, since we are compelled to wait for the world revolution. There is no other way open to us of raising our technique to the modern level.

At another point in his report, Lenin stated: ". . . owing to the economic situation the Soviet power is shaking."

Calvert's essay

Calvert's boundless goodwill toward the Soviet Republic and his faith in industrial unionism, strengthened by his experience in the IWW, came together. He had been hearing for years that workers did not need capitalists to make factories run. He had been a department foreman in the Ford plant, so he could speak with some knowledge about the abilities of workers to organize production. He also knew engineers who sympathized with the Russian revolution. What American workers could do in the United States they could also do in the Soviet Republic, given the opportunity. Why not recruit workers and engineers in the United States to come to the Soviet Republic with their skills and their tools to put into practice the principles of workers' sovereignty in industry? The long Marxist tradition of class solidarity across national frontiers underwrote the impulse to draw on international working-class support to aid the Soviet Republic in its crisis and its challenge.

Lenin had already indicated his respect for American workers and his confidence that they would give support to the Soviet Republic in the spirit of international class solidarity. In 1919 Lenin had sent Ludwig K. Martens to the United States with the general task of finding, tapping and channeling that support. Martens had established a Society for Technical Aid to Soviet Russia, first in New York City and then in several other large cities. His presence provoked indignation in the United States Congress. President Wilson had fixed the political line towards the new Soviet Republic by calling it "the pariah among nations" and assuring Congress that he did not intend to deal with the Bolsheviks. A committee of Congress held hearings to publicize Martens's activities and succeeded in having him deported in 1920.

Calvert had heard, nevertheless, that some 25,000 Americans had registered with Martens's Society for Technical Aid, indicating their willingness to help the Soviet Republic survive. He also knew that unemployment was high in the United States and that this would be a factor making it easier to find recruits for overseas work.

Calvert was told that approximately 1,000 Russian-Americans had returned from the United States and were presently in the Soviet Republic waiting for work. He thought it important that these returning immigrants, many of them experienced in American production techniques, be organized, kept together and employed in modern conditions.

Calvert began talking about his idea with delegates at the Hotel Lux and found the response encouraging. It seemed to fit the times and the needs. Lenin had detailed Mikhail Markovich Borodin to live at the Lux as his contact with the foreign delegates: "Lenin's eyes and ears," someone said. Borodin thought Calvert's idea important enough to be brought to Lenin's attention and he suggested that Calvert set it down on paper. In April Calvert delivered to Borodin his essay entitled "Economic Reconstruction". This Borodin sent or delivered to Lenin, who returned it a few days later having written diagonally across the first page with a bold red pencil: "A good idea. Give us something definite."

Calvert threw himself into the project with renewed energy. He became known as the man whose idea had Lenin's support. Borodin jokingly gave him the nickname, "come on, let's go", a phrase constantly heard from Calvert.

When Bill Haywood arrived in Moscow in May, 1921, he was also installed at the Lux. Haywood the celebrity was of course well known to Calvert; and Calvert was not unknown to Haywood, since Calvert's wife, Mellie, had worked for a time as Haywood's secretary in the Chicago IWW office. As soon as Haywood read Calvert's paper, he added his own overflowing enthusiasm to Calvert's. American workers building and running an industry in the Soviet Republic! This was made to order for Big Bill Haywood, and he let it be known he wanted to get aboard as the project gathered momentum. He had come as a refugee for an indefinite stay, and, as he said, "This is something I can do".

Rutgers's article

About June 1st Rutgers also arrived at the Lux as a delegate to the Third Congress of the Communist International. As we have seen, he too had been mulling the economic predicament of the Soviet Republic, something he had observed first hand in 1918 and 1919 while working in the Soviet department of water transportation. He was gravely concerned by the decision of the Soviet leaders to make even temporary "concession agreements" with foreign capitalists. He thought these neither desirable nor necessary, and the alternative he proposed was remarkably similar to the ideas of Calvert. That Rutgers had come to his views independently of Calvert is clear from the date of publication of his article "Industrial Labor Colonies", published on June 1, 1921, in the Moscow organ of the Third Congress of the Communist International. He must have had it written for delivery on arrival in Moscow. Since ideas are a reflection of reality, it is not so surprising that different minds were thinking along the same lines.

In his article Rutgers wrote:

> The question arises, whether foreign labor, upon which concessions would have to be based largely anyhow, could not achieve results without the help of foreign capitalists. This question presents itself with more force, since a large number of American-Russian workers, partly trained in the highly developed American machine-industry, loudly and insistently claim admittance to Soviet Russia. There is little doubt that any amount of American labor of different degrees of skill and specialization could be had and that no serious obstacles exist in having American technical and managing specialists join the exodus. It certainly is not the American capitalist we are most anxious to get.

Rutgers was proposing this to the delegates to the Congress of the Communist International. He urged them to consider putting the suggestion into practice in their different countries with the aim of generating an emigration of pioneers of good technical and moral qualities from all industrially developed countries to the Soviet Republic. He added:

> ... the economic reconstruction of Russia is so all important that it must be considered a vital part of communist propaganda to further this experiment, once it will be decided upon by our Russian friends.

It was not long before Haywood had brought Calvert and Rutgers together. They exchanged papers. Each had something valuable to share with the other. Calvert had the scrawled encouragement from Lenin to move forward on the idea; Rutgers had experience in the Soviet Republic and was a Communist, trusted and respected by Lenin.

The first two weeks of June were a time of feverish activity for Calvert and Rutgers. Lenin had said he wanted something definite. That would require fixing on a specific project in a specific region, and for that it was essential to have facts about resources and facilities. Calvert had engaged the interest of Malkin, a Communist who worked in a foreign trade bureau. He made the third, a vital Soviet member, in an ad hoc committee with Calvert and Rutgers. The latter two agreed to drop their activities in connection with the RILU Congress and the Third Congress of the Communist International in order to be able to devote full time to developing a proposal.

Borodin was fully supportive, a sign of Lenin's continuing interest. So were other Soviet Communists, especially Simon (Cy) Berg, who had lived in the United States and was head of bakeries in Moscow at the time; Shlyapnikov, head of the Metal Workers Union; and Lipschutz, an employee of the security forces, who had belonged to the IWW before joining the Communist Party.

Calvert's effectiveness was handicapped by the fact that he did not speak Russian, so Borodin with Berg's help procured an interpreter and assigned him to assist Calvert. The man chosen, Charlie Maskalunas, was an Estonian worker who had lived in the state of Washington, had joined the IWW in 1917, and had been deported from Seattle for his activity in the lumber camps of the Northwest. He had arrived in Petrograd in time to join the Communist Party and take part in the defense of the October Revolution, for which he was awarded a Red Star. He not only interpreted, he supplemented Calvert's advocacy of the enterprise as they were discussing it with Soviet officials and bureaucrats. He and Calvert became warm comrades or, in Calvert's still purist IWW terminology, "fellow workers".

One of the bureaucrats was Fedorovich, an engineer in the Department of Coal Administration of all Russia. He was in possession of a rare report, known as "the red book", on coal and iron deposits in the Kuznetsk Basin, and he refused to let go of it for any reason. This was the first of many problems created for the new enterprise by the old-guard engineers entrenched in industry and government bureaus. After several rebuffs Rutgers was finally allowed to study the report under the watchful eye of Fedorovich and copy down some data.

Rutgers reported progress to his friend, Nikolai Ivanovich Bukharin, who repeated that Lenin was interested and wanted a definite proposal.

With the help of his interpreter, Calvert talked with miners from Siberia who were in Moscow for the RILU Congress. Their information fortified the growing predilection for the Kuznetsk Basin and fixed the focus on Kemerovo, which, they reported, had an abundance of good quality coal, water and rail transport, timber resources not far away and rich agricultural land.

The three-man ad hoc committee then met with the entire Siberian delegation, including Suchkyov, a member of the Siberian Revolutionary Committee, which was struggling to establish its authority over the vast region where pacification following the civil war was still precarious and incomplete. These meetings won over Suchkyov and crystallized a plan to visit and inspect the Kuznetsk Basin to locate the best possible site for an American industrial colony.

A definite proposal

Rutgers began work on a letter to Lenin "with something definite". He and Calvert went over it point by point.

As background, Rutgers restated the arguments he had set forth in his article on industrial colonies: (1) It is necessary to develop modern big industry, "the indispensable basis for solidifying the proletarian revolution". (2) Concessions to foreign capitalists are not certain either to be accepted or to be satisfactory in their results. (3) Russia can utilize foreign experience and training in modern industries without participation by capitalist concessionaires. (4) Workers in the highly developed countries clamor for immigration into Russia, partly for idealistic reasons, partly to escape unemployment. (5) Groups of foreign workers cannot be utilized in existing industries, because raw materials cannot be assured nor can the absorption of output in later steps in the production process. (6) Therefore such groups should work directly from natural resources and produce something for immediate use. (7) These conditions will best be realized in an industry based on the production of food and the exploitation of wood, coal and iron, so as to produce such items as agricultural machinery.

The letter then stated a concrete proposal: the colonization of Kuznetsk Basin. The advantages of the region with its unlimited resources in food, wood, coal and iron were described. The richness of coal of high quality was the main feature. Coal deposits were estimated at four times those of the Donets Basin, yet its production in 1914 had been only 1/32 of the Donets. The coal had a high caloric value with a low percentage of ash and sulfur. It was therefore ideal for the production of coke, which meant that it could serve as the basis for a metallurgical industry. "As to transport, part of the region is crossed by the Kuznetsk Railroad, whereas the River Tom connects the Eastern part of the region with Tomsk, and via the Ob River and its affluents, to the Urals. For local transport, horses can be used and raised, since there is a big crop of oats."

The main purpose of the colonization was the development of the region into "an industrial unit". But that would require years. The letter also stressed some more immediate results.

The great Trans–Siberian Railroad was running only four to six trains a day in each direction. Locomotives were standing cold for lack of coal. Some connecting lines to the Trans-Siberian were not worked at all. "The immediate results," wrote Rutgers, "would be to increase the production of coal, of which in the first period only a small part will be used for development of the region. This increased coal production will enable the Siberian Railroad and its connecting lines to improve transport, which will mean more food to European Russia."

Rutgers then dealt with the question of control over this proposed colony of foreigners and its relationship to the Soviet Republic. He had scorn for the old Russian bureaucracy and was sure that its maddening inefficiency had roots in persistent ill will and intentional sabotage by enemies of the revolution. At the same time, it was clear the colony could not be totally independent of Soviet authority. His proposed solution was a Board of Management of three members, to be appointed by the Council of People's Commissars of the Soviet Republic (*not* elected by the colonists). This Board would "have a free hand in the internal affairs of the colony, especially as regards industrial organization and economic measures". The members of the Board would be subject to recall at any time by the Council of People's Commissars. The Rutgers proposal left no doubt that the colony was, in the final analysis, to be subject to Soviet proletarian rule, as administered through the Soviet Republic.

The Board would undertake to provide the colonists with housing, food, education and recreation "as near as possible to foreign standards." The Soviet Government would yearly put at the disposal of the Board the amount of money necessary, partly in rubles, partly in foreign currency, to conduct its affairs. Colonists and other foreign sympathizers would be asked to contribute to the foreign currency fund. "We will appeal to the American workers who want to come to Kuznetsk to contribute their savings, estimated at two hundred dollars above the cost of transport." In another passage which shows the magnitude of the enterprise Rutgers envisaged, he wrote: "If ten thousand workers pay five hundred each, this means a capital of six million dollars". (There was either a mathematical or a typographical error in that excited calculation.) Amounts advanced by the Soviet Government would be covered by products of the colony or "remain as a deficit on its account". The Board of Management would be allowed to dispose of one–half its surplus production for further development within the region.

The immediate next step, according to the letter, should be a survey of the Kuznetsk region by a party "of about a dozen mostly American workers and experts". Their task would be "to list whatever is required now and in the near future for the development of the Unit". They would submit a report. Rutgers was impatient to begin: "This expedition should not wait until the end of the Congress, since quick action is necessary. . ." but Lenin's support for the project was felt to be indispensable. Rutgers even made this a condition on his proposal: "The proposers consider it only possible to go ahead, if they have your wholehearted personal support in this matter". Perhaps Rutgers foresaw that impossible problems of coordination with the Soviet Government would arise if Lenin himself was not fully committed to overcoming all difficulties.

Martens's reluctance

Rutgers and Bukharin, with whom Rutgers was consulting, knew that Lenin would pay heed to the views of Martens in a matter concerning technical aid from the United States, since Martens had gained valuable first-hand experience in his previous assignment. Therefore Rutgers and Calvert took the Rutgers letter to Martens and asked him to join them in signing it. Martens was very reluctant to do so. This was doubtless due to an opinion he had formed of Calvert and would soon express to Lenin. In the project that was taking shape, Calvert would obviously become the principal recruiter and organizer in the United States (Haywood could not safely return). Martens found Calvert too garrulous, ebullient, unreliable, shallow. Perhaps Martens also foresaw difficulties for Calvert on the American front because of his single-minded loyalty to the IWW. Heated polemics between some IWWs and some Communists were continuing at the RILU Congress.

Further, at the Tenth Congress of the Russian Communist Party (Bolshevik), (March 8 to 16, 1921) a majority had approved a resolution, drafted and supported by Lenin, which characterized as "a syndicalist and anarchist deviation" certain theses similar to those of the IWW. A polarization was taking place in Left labor circles in the United States, and there was some question as to whether the IWW would continue to support the Soviet Republic. Would Calvert, an IWW, be able to develop a strong, unified organization in the United States with full Communist Party support? There was reason for doubt.

Finally, though, Martens also signed, and the letter or "thesis" of June 12, 1921, with the three signatures, Rutgers, Calvert and Martens, was delivered in great haste to the desk of Bukharin. There it remained for eight days while Calvert and Rutgers fretted and waited for an answer from Lenin. Finally they called on

Bukharin who, for the first time, discovered the letter addressed to Lenin among his papers. He rushed to the telephone and in the presence of the other two explained to Lenin what had happened. This episode produced an interesting rebuke of Martens by Lenin. (Did Lenin suspect that Martens had deviously caused the delay?) In a letter dated June 22, 1921, addressed to Martens, Lenin wrote:

Comrade Martens,

I must reproach you for sending the papers about the American colonies in Russia through the wrong channels.

I read them only on June 20. You should not have sent them through Bukharin, but should have set out the proposals in Russian, about 20 lines all told, and sent them on to the Council of Labour and Defense, with a personal copy for me and a brief letter.

The delay was due to the records being sent through the wrong channels.

Now about the substance of the matter. I am in favour, *if* the American workers and settlers in general will bring along:

1) Food supplies for two years (you write that this has been done before, which means that it can be done again);

2) Clothing for the same period;

3) Implements of labour.

Point 1 (and 2) are the most important. The $200 are less important. Given Point 1, I agree to *support* the project *in every way*.

In order to expedite matters, please make a draft C.L.D. resolution and hand it in at the C.L.D. today (before 3 p.m., if you can make it). We shall decide at 6 p.m. today; if you cannot make it, hand it in at the C.L.D. at 6 p.m. anyway, we shall set up a commission and decide on Friday, June 24.

The draft resolution: (1) the terms—the three listed above; (2) management (you + one American worker + 1 man from the People's Commissariat for Labour?); (3) our assistance (we provide the land, timber, mines, etc.); (4) financial terms (specify).

Please reply by bearer.

> V. Ulyanov (Lenin)
> Chairman, Council
> of People's Commissars

P.S. After writing this letter I discovered that the question was on today's C.L.D. agenda. Please work out the points I have indicated (*Lenin on the United States*, 1970, 541).

Apparently Martens carried out these instructions. Calvert and

Rutgers were given a copy of a "Decision of the Council of Labor and Defense on the American Industrial Immigration" dated June 22, 1921, and signed by Lenin as Chairman. It provided in its opening paragraph:

> To pronounce desirable the development of certain industrial enterprises by way of turning them over to groups of American workers, or industrially developed peasants, on conditions which will guarantee to them a certain degree of economic autonomy.

This was the first time the word "autonomy" had been employed to characterize the projected colonies. Its appearance was very gratifying to Rutgers and Calvert. The phrase that soon became current and later led to some confusion and dispute was "Autonomous Industrial Colony Kuzbas," the last word being a contracted form of Kuznetsk Basin.

On-the-spot survey

The C.L.D. "Decision" also provided that "Comrade Rutgers and his co-workers" were to be provided the means to visit the Urals and the Kuznetsk Basin for the purpose of their on-the-spot survey. Lenin's secretary, Gorbunov, provided requisitions for a private railway car and supplies for the journey. Rutgers and Calvert assembled the following party to accompany them:

Bronka Kornblitt, stenographer to Rutgers

Charlie Maskalunas, interpreter

Emil Feltman, an IWW member, a German-American with 30 years of experience as a miner in the United States.

Grescia Skolnik

A. A. Heller, a Communist Party member who had worked with the Society for Technical Aid to Soviet Russia.

The last two were named to the party by Martens. It was agreed that Haywood should remain in Moscow to promote the project among the many foreign delegates who were attending the Third Congress of the Communist International, which had opened on June 22nd.

Joined to form part of the Moscow–Novo–Nikolaevsk Express, the party in its private railroad car departed Moscow on June 28, 1921. They were accompanied by two armed Red Guards against the possibility of a military assault by one of the bands still occasionally reported active in the area to be traversed. A crisis developed when the train crew of engineer and two firemen wanted to drop the private car in an effort to lighten the load. The "express" was steadily losing time. Maskalunas, the advocate-interpreter, saved the day and converted the three Russian trainmen to support for an American colony at Kuzbas. They were burning green wood in their engine and yearned for real coal.

At Yekaterinberg in the Urals they stopped long enough to visit the room where the Tsar's family had been executed. Their guide had no doubt that this "military measure" was necessary "to eliminate the cement of opposition to the revolution". There could be no turning back.

Everywhere they saw signs of economic disorganization and paralysis. Their paper rubles were practically worthless. For money they used black bread brought from Moscow. Near Omsk they acquired poods of salt to use as a medium of exchange at later stops. Typhus was widespread. It had already taken the life of thousands, among them the American journalist John Reed, so Rutgers and Calvert agreed to reduce the risk by denying admission to the curious and random visitors at their car. With revolutionary rigor this was even applied to two female stowaways who were riding the rails to the University at Tomsk.

On July 5th the group reached Novo–Nikolaevsk (later renamed Novosibirsk, "New Siberia") on the River Ob. Here the Siberian Revolutionary Committee had its seat in a high school. Smirnov, the head of the Committee, was absent on an inspection trip. In charge was Suchkyov, who had already been won over in Moscow. The Siberian Revolutionary Committee thereafter provided the group with every possible assistance in making its tour of the region.

At Yurga the private car was detached from its train on the Trans–Siberian and transferred to a train on the Kuznetsk Railway. At Kolchugina (now Leninsk) they were joined by Smirnov. Then followed visits to Prokopevsk and the Guriev Works, where they inspected mines and smelting furnaces. Smirnov then returned to his headquarters for work on a proposed agreement to present to Rutgers and Calvert. He assigned to them as escort Baravov, a Communist worker from a Petrograd factory who had been sent with his wife to help organize Soviet power in Siberia. He was on the political committee charged with overseeing the Kemerovo mines.

With Baravov they proceeded to Kemerovo. They were pleasantly surprised at its advanced state of development. To Calvert the enthusiast it looked "like Gary, Indiana, in the heart of Siberia". A coal mine was being worked with facilities installed by the French and Belgian corporation, Kopikus, before the revolution. Four impressive seams of coal were visible. There were housing accommodations for eleven thousand people. One particularly commodious structure had housed the White Guard General Kolchak and his staff during the Civil War. A generator provided the town with electric lights, and a pumping station provided running water taken from the River Tom. On the bluff stood a small Orthodox church. On the west bank of the river they visited a chemical plant still under construction by a crew of some four hundred workers. It seemed to be approximately eighty percent completed. Hopes were expressed that it would be started up in a few months, using coal from the mine as raw material.

From Kemerovo the party proceeded by steamer on the River Tom to Kuznetsk. Many signs of coal seams were observed, confirming the reports of rich reserves. The surrounding countryside was being used for raising wheat and cattle. In the ports they found cheese, butter and honey. On board were entrepreneurs (some of them ex–prisoners of war) who had come with handicrafts to trade for foodstuffs. This was a region that could feed an enormous crowd of workers. The Siberian summer contributed to the euphoria.

At Tomsk they saw the university, the only one in Siberia and, with 6,000 students, the fourth largest in Russia. Its laboratories drew favorable comment from the engineer Rutgers. He foresaw its services to an industrial colony. Also in the city they saw a glass factory, a tannery, a shoe factory and brick kilns, all of which they added to their wish list to be discussed with Smirnov.

Siberian Revolutionary Committee

The tour completed, the party returned to Novo–Nikolaevsk, where it spent the next eight days in negotiations and in drafting agreements. The Siberian Revolutionary Committee could not have been more cooperative. It prepared a "Schema of Mutual Relations Between the SibRevCom and the Immigration of American and Other Foreign Workers to the Kuznetsk Coal and Iron

Basin." This draft proposal was forwarded to the C.L.D. in Moscow and became one of its working documents as a final agreement was being prepared. It stated the willingness of SibRevCom to place at the disposal of the "Immigrant Unit": the Kemerovo coal deposits; 25,000 acres of farmland; the chemical works, brick kilns and sawmills in Kemerovo; brick kilns, tannery and shoe factory in Tomsk; logs to be delivered to Kemerovo in the spring of 1922 for the building of additional housing; rail and water transport; clay, sand, lime, cement and pig iron; food rations (*pyok*) in accordance with rules established for analogous categories of Russian workmen; sheepskin and felt boots for the winter 1922–23.

The number of American workers to be received in 1922 was estimated at 2,800.

As its crowning gesture of goodwill the SibRevCom put on display royal jewelry confiscated from various passengers fleeing east on the Trans–Siberian Railway. This was to be sent to Moscow with the request that it be converted into a fund for the purchase of machinery for the Immigrant Unit. Its value was estimated at $200,000.

To assist the Siberian Revolutionary Committee with preparations to receive the first contingent, and at the Committee's request, Feltman, the German-American miner, and Maskalunas, the interpreter and lumber worker, remained in Novo–Nikolaevsk when the rest of the party departed for Moscow. This proved a real privation for Calvert. He had lost his faithful channel of communication with Russians.

At Omsk the party came upon a group of American immigrants headed for Moscow. On hearing the plans for Kuzbas sixteen of them, all lumber workers, returned to Novo–Nikolaevsk and Kemerovo in order to prepare a lumber camp on the River Tom and cut wood during the winter to be used in Kemerovo construction. The SibRevCom promised to supply them with tools, warm clothes and food. Thus with a high degree of fraternity, spontaneity, local initiative and boundless confidence in the future, a vanguard of the vanguard cheerfully went to its newly discovered task. Something like this vision had drawn them to the Soviet Republic, and now they had happily stumbled into the beginnings of its realization!

On the return trip the party laid over for two weeks in the Urals while Rutgers and Calvert studied the resources and facilities in the Bogoslovsk region. They contemplated the ultimate linkage of the coal and coke resources of Kuzbas with the iron of the Urals. Calvert prepared a report on his visit to Nadezhdinsk Works, the region's most important blast furnace of iron and steel (now the city of Serov). Rutgers was now working on his report of the survey to the C.L.D., and in it he included his vision of the coordination between the two regions in building a production enterprise of vast potential. He was confirmed in his belief that this could be a source of machinery for socialist agriculture. The factory at the Nadezhdinsk Works, with much wonderful equipment standing idle, "can produce almost anything needed for further expansion". Here "any American worker or specialist would feel perfectly at home", he wrote.

The private railway car was left at Yekaterinberg, because Martens was due to arrive on a survey of his own in the Urals and would take it over with his group. Calvert, Rutgers and company returned to Moscow by regular train, arriving on September 4, 1921.

Rutgers–Calvert Report

Meanwhile, back at the Hotel Lux, Haywood had recruited some new activists to give their time and support to the new enterprise:

Tom Barker, born in England, an emigrant to Australia where he joined the IWW and became editor of an IWW newspaper; author of *Story of the Sea*, highly valued by maritime workers; leader of a general strike in New Zealand; labor organizer in South America.

Tom Mann, a well-known English labor leader, active in a big railroad strike of the transport workers union.

Nat Watkins, English, a leader in the coal miners' union.

Jack Beyer, an American Indian, a member and officer of the IWW, a co-defendant with Haywood in the Chicago trial for "criminal syndicalism".

Rutgers's report to the C.L.D., prepared with the assistance of Calvert, was soon ready and it was signed by Rutgers on September 12, 1921. It proposed colonization by Americans of Kuznetsk Basin and the Bogoslovsk region in the Urals. The estimate of the number of American immigrants to be expected in Kuzbas in 1922 had been changed to four thousand. The Soviet Government was asked to provide transportation for that number from the Soviet frontier to their destination. For the purchase of "agricultural and other machinery" for the Colony at Kuzbas a credit of $200,000 was requested of C.L.D. Rutgers added:

> As a more general proposition, the Soviet Government is asked to acknowledge the extreme importance of this form of labor colonization by granting a dollar for every dollar that the American industrial colonists, as far as they participate in the creation of Soviet state enterprises, put up for buying tools and machinery. It is figured that in average each colonist will spend $100 for this purpose, in addition to paying his traveling expenses [to the Soviet frontier] and $100 for extra food and clothes.

Under this "more general proposition" the credit from the Soviet Government for machinery purposes would depend on still uncertain factors, the number of colonists and the amount of their own contribution. So, for the purpose of planning a beginning, Rutgers in his summary repeated the figure of $200,000 as the Soviet hard currency credit sought for the Kuzbas Colony. Another $100,000 was requested for a similar colony at the Nadezhdinsk Works in the Urals.

In addition, a sum of $5,000 was requested for use by a recruiting and organizing committee in the United States. A crucial paragraph specifically named Calvert as the man to organize the American committee. Here is what the Rutgers–Calvert document stated (over Rutgers's signature) on an issue that was known to be troubling Martens:

> It is suggested that H. S. Calvert, who took part in our mission, and who is a member of the IWW in the ranks of which we will have to find most of the revolutionary elements willing and capable of achieving the aim, be entrusted to form a committee of three in America to organize in America, in co-operation with the general immigration committee, the necessary labor and directing forces and to purchase the necessary implements and materials. It may be remembered that Comrade Calvert signed, together with Martens and myself, the original propositions to Lenin and that he advocated the ideas of the present suggestions already in the United States. Calvert has the complete confidence of Haywood and myself.

". . . the IWW in the ranks of which we will have to find most of the revolutionary elements": could the Communist, Rutgers, have drafted those lines? He signed, so of course he, too, was responsible for them. They sound like the composition of an IWW enthusiast, tainted with sectarianism. The passage was bound to confirm Martens in his misgivings and therefore to create an obstacle for Lenin.

Thus Rutgers and Calvert laid before Lenin and the C.L.D., as one (unnecessary) detail in a general proposal to create the Colony, the thorny issue of Calvert's future role. The inference is strong that Calvert was anxious to nail down his prerogative. His was the only assignment specifically mentioned. Note that a committee of three was contemplated for the United States. This also became an issue in the C.L.D.

The report incorporated the "Schema" already worked out with the Siberian Revolutionary Committee and recommended its approval. Rutgers and Calvert repeated that the Colony would be "under the continuous supervision of the Russian Soviet Government" which "will have at any time the possibility to disapprove of the actions of the Management and recall them".

Haywood Resolution

There is no reason to suppose that Haywood took any part in the actual preparation of this report. He referred to it as "the report by Comrades Rutgers and Calvert." But he does now come on the scene with a "Resolution" which he signed and most probably drafted. It was also signed by Tom Mann, Tom Barker and J. H. Beyer. This Resolution served to convey to Lenin Haywood's strong support for the proposal. It was incorporated as an appendix to the Rutgers–Calvert report. This "Haywood Resolution" opened with some "whereas" clauses:

> Whereas, we consider that such a form of organization as suggested, combining as it does the essential structure of the capitalist corporation and of industrial management by the Industrial Workers of the World and other revolutionary industrial forces, will be much more productive, much more economical, and much more satisfactory than that of any private concessionaire, and

> Whereas, we believe that a concerted economic plan will throw the full force of the trained, skilled, technical, western workers into one front fully concentrated, instead of dissipating their energies and knowledge through the backward economic forces in European Russia, and will produce tremendous results, and create a central system for increasing from time to time the sphere and field of influence of the proposed unit, etc.

This Resolution indicates how Haywood saw the industrial colony of advanced workers from abroad as a natural adaptation of the industrial union to conditions in an underdeveloped country. Development of the Soviet Republic was a responsibility of all advanced workers whatever their nationality; it was "their" country. This internationalist view would have pleased Marx and must have pleased Lenin. The Resolution concluded:

> Resolved, that we assure the C.L.D. that this plan will meet with a splendid response amongst the revolutionary industrial workers of the world, who will in the main finance their own journeys and bring supplies of small and necessary tools to follow their own occupations, in order to work out a new economic plan suitable to the workers of all countries.

Interview with Lenin

The Rutgers–Calvert report of September 12, 1921, with its various appendices apparently reached Lenin without delay. On September 19th he received in his office for a discussion of the project the three who had now emerged as its principal proponents: Rutgers, Calvert and Haywood. Lenin greeted Rutgers warmly as an old comrade. Haywood, whom he had also received earlier in the summer, was "Big Bill". Having heard from Borodin, no doubt, that Calvert rejected the title "Comrade", Lenin pointedly greeted him in the IWW style with "Fellow worker". The interview was carried on in English, with Rutgers helping Lenin now and then to find the word he sought.

A letter from Lenin to Valerian V. Kuibyshev dated September 19th gives Lenin's summary of this discussion. Following are excerpts:

> Comrade Kuibyshev,
>
> I have just had a call from Rutgers, Calvert and Haywood representing the American workers colony group who wish to take the Nadezhdinsk Works and *several* enterprises in Kuznetsk basin.
>
> They want their representative (with an interpreter) to attend the Council of Labor and Defense on Friday. I think we should let them come.
>
> I also draw your attention to and request you to inform all members of the commission and subcommissions of the following:
>
> 1) The Nadezhdinsk Works, in their opinion, is both economically and technically connected with a group of enterprises in Kuzbas, for it will

provide tractors for their farms; tractors and all other farming implements for the peasants; repair of machinery for their group's enterprises in Kuzbas, etc., equipment for water transport, communications
with Siberia, etc.

2) In Kuznetsk basin they are taking 12,000 dessiatines of land [about
32,000 acres] and *several* enterprises, wishing to set up a large and
complete economic whole.

3) They want *only* 300,000 dollars in cash. It would be wrong to think
otherwise.

4) In addition they want grain and clothing, in order to start the
necessary building operations *at once*. They say work should be started
this very winter to have time to finish it by the spring of 1922.

5) They stress that they will have a clearcut administrative set-up for
their workers' group; and the whole group (3,000–6,000 workers) selected from among the *best* workers, mostly young and unmarried men,
who have had *practical* experience in their line, and had lived in a climate similar to that of Russia (Canada and the Northern United States).

6) They want to be directly subordinate to the Council of Labor and
Defense. Something like an autonomous state trust consisting of a
workers' association (ibid. 549).

The Soviet Government had to consider carefully the financial
risk it would be taking if it approved the proposed colony or
colonies. The Rutgers–Calvert report had contained an ambiguity
on that point. Apparently in the discussions in Lenin's office on
September 19th, the ambiguity had been resolved; hence Lenin's
insistence that "they want *only* $300,000 in cash". In a second
letter to Kuibyshev, dated September 22nd, Lenin urged the importance of an "extremely precise" contract, "drawn up by our
own *lawyer* (a Communist)." He clearly wanted to minimize the
risk of misunderstanding between the parties in this novel enterprise. He also insisted on the importance of "a reliable *interpreter* who knows both languages *well*" (ibid. 551).

The pledge drafted by Lenin

The practical genius of Lenin, his ability to go right to the heart
of a new problem, stands forth in a short document he enclosed in
that second letter to Kuibyshev. It was a pledge he himself had
drafted as he weighed the possibilities and the potential problems
involved in bringing foreign workers from an advanced country
into the trying material and social conditions of backward and

devastated Russia. Character, dedication and morale were going to be of enormous importance in making these colonies a success. The pledge was a warning to candidates for the colonies that the demands on them would be extraordinary. It was a winnowing tool. It was also Lenin's little homily to every candidate, worthy of frequent review, a kind of *credo* that summed up the human relationships he sought to cultivate between colonists and the Soviet people. Every American worker going to Russia would have to sign the following pledge:

1. We pledge ourselves to arrange and *collectively* guarantee that only men willing and able consciously to bear the hardships inevitable in the rehabilitation of industry in a very backward and incredibly devastated country *will arrive* in Russia.

2. Those coming to Russia pledge themselves to work with maximum intensiveness and with productivity of labour and discipline on a higher level than capitalist standards, otherwise Russia will be unable to outstrip or even catch up with capitalism.

3. We pledge ourselves to refer all conflicts without exception, whatever their nature, to the final decision of the supreme Soviet power in Russia and conscientiously to abide by all its decisions.

4. We pledge to bear in mind the extreme nervousness of the starved and exhausted Russian workers and peasants in the vicinity of our enterprise and to help them in every way to establish friendly relations and overcome suspicion and envy (ibid. 551–2: This English version differs somewhat from the version carried by Calvert to the U.S.; see Appendix B.).

The Martens problem

It appears from these letters and the pledge that Lenin had decided that the Rutgers–Calvert–Haywood proposal should be supported in principle. Now the question of Martens's opposition comes to the fore. Martens was in the Urals on an assignment. Apparently he sent a telegram expressing reservations and asking that a decision be delayed until his return to Moscow. Lenin referred to this in a telegram to Martens on September 27th. The Council of Labor and Defense had met on September 23rd with Rutgers present. As Lenin had recommended, the Council decided it was desirable to conclude an agreement with the American group, making facilities in Kuzbas and the Urals (Nadezhdinsk Works) available for industrial colonies. A commission was named to negotiate a final agreement with Rutgers, Haywood and Calvert. Lenin wrote the following telegram on September 27th:

Yekaterinburg

Telegraph Martens [in] Nizhny Tagil that Rutgers insists on an immediate decision on the matter of leasing a part of Kuznetsk basin and the Nadezhdinsk Works to the group of American workers saying the urgency springs from the need for a representative of Calvert's group to go to America immediately. I am at a loss, in view of your request to put it off until your return, for I should not like to decide without you. Let us know: first, when you are arriving in Moscow; second, your opinion in essence of Rutger's haste; do you believe it absolutely imperative to make an immediate decision or advise to insist that Rutgers should await your return? In spite of your telegram Rutgers says that you agree with him.

Lenin

(ibid., 553).

Lenin learned that Martens was to return to Moscow on October 15th. Rutgers and Calvert did not want to await his return before concluding an agreement; perhaps they saw in Martens's absence a convenient opportunity to circumvent his opposition. But Lenin continued to insist that Martens should be heard. On September 29th, Lenin wrote to Leon Trotsky as follows:

We have decided now (7:30 p.m.) in the C.L.D. to call Martens immediately, not October 15th, in the name of C.L.D. Comrade Rutgers made a wild speech, saying "We do not want to wait. We yield to saboteurs. We are not working for the sake of money, etc." Comrade Rutgers's excitement compelled us to yield (We wanted to wait until October 15th, Martens's day of arrival). It would be important if Comrade Trotsky personally influenced Comrade Rutgers not to leave, not to be nervous, but to wait for Martens. (I am afraid someone associated with Rutgers is afraid of Martens's criticism.)

(Martens thinks Calvert is not solid, that Haywood is half anarchist, and that Rutgers is a wonderful comrade, a propagandist, but hardly an administrator. Such are the leading three.)

Lenin

(Lenin, *Sobranie Sochineniia* (Collected Works), 53:231).

On October 11th Kuibyshev sent Lenin the draft of an agreement as proposed by the Soviet negotiating commission and approved by the Presidium of the Supreme Economic Council. The ambiguity as to the Soviet financial commitment was still there, so Lenin objected. Furthermore, Lenin now expressed dissatisfaction with the composition of the prospective leading group (Rutgers, Calvert, Haywood). Perhaps Martens had arrived and scored some points. Between October 12 and 15th, Lenin wrote the following letter to members of the Politburo of the Central Committee:

> In my opinion we cannot accept Rutgers's proposals now, in their present shape. But let's try the following: make him *alter the group* (Rutgers + Haywood + Calvert). And amend the financial terms. I suggest the following resolution:
>
> Rejecting Comrade Rutgers's proposals in their present form, i.e., the proposals of Comrade Bogdanov and the members of the Supreme Economic Council Presidium who voted with him.
>
> The Central Committee (followed by the Council of Labour and Defense, as is the Soviet practice) expresses the insistent desire that Comrade Rutgers's group should not regard this refusal as final, but should rework its proposals on the following principles: (a) change the composition of the group of initiators, by co-opting 5–8 prominent members of the American trade union movement or other labour organizations; (b) reduce our government's expenditures down to a maximum of $300,000; (c) reduce and specify our expenditures in the event the contract is cancelled.
>
> Lenin
>
> (*Lenin on U.S.*, 1970, 555).

In a letter to Martens dated October 15, 1921, Lenin again insisted that "Rutgers's plan must be corrected . . . and not just rejected" (ibid. 559).

Lenin's idea

Lenin was fighting to save the proposal to establish American labor industrial colonies. Yet, unlike Rutgers, he did not see this as the sole and sufficient means of tapping the techniques and experience of advanced capitalist countries. He regarded Rutgers's condemnation of concessions to foreign capitalist companies as a symptom of excessive "leftism". Lenin had not changed his view, expressed at the Tenth Congress of the Bolshevik Party, that "concessions are necessary". He still deplored the fact that the Soviet Government had been unable to negotiate a single concession agreement with a foreign capitalist company. He was continually seeking to gather some benefits from the decree of November 23, 1920, which he had hailed as "a step towards establishing relations with a view to granting concessions".

The ability of Lenin to promote progress along both these tracks at once stands out in the negotiations of October, 1921. Julius Hammer, an American millionaire born in Russia, indicated he was prepared to give workers of the Urals region one million poods of grain on easy terms (5%) and to take produce from the Urals (e.g. asbestos) for sale on commission in the United States (ibid. 558). Lenin seized on this as the opportunity he had been waiting for. Through Martens he learned that Hammer's son (Armand J. Hammer) was interested in helping to rehabilitate industry in the Urals. To Lenin it was politically very important to show the world that foreign capitalists were beginning to negotiate concessions with the Soviet Republic. At the same time, the Rutgers–Calvert proposal for developing the Nadezhdinsk Works in the Urals was under consideration by the Soviet authorities.

To Lenin these two opportunities did not exclude each other. On October 15th Lenin wrote to Martens asking if Hammer could be persuaded to undertake the financing of the Rutgers group, "to save the Urals and *improve* the composition of the group? by including, say, four American *businessmen?*" (ibid. 559.) He urged Martens to *correct* Rutgers's plan by bringing in the two capitalists, the Hammers. This must have made Rutgers's hair stand on end. And it was of course contrary to the IWW rhetoric beloved of Haywood and Calvert, in which capitalists were mentioned only to be belabored. Lenin's proposal was totally incongruous with what they had in mind.

Viewed in retrospect, this proposal of Lenin's helps to point up a contrast between him and the other three principals. He had emerged from an underdeveloped country and felt, as they never could, the curse of backwardness. He had a Marxist's appreciation of the revolutionary role that capitalism had played in developing production in Western Europe and the United States. In the backward conditions of Russia and Siberia such enterprise would be a stimulus and a carrier of progress. Production of the most advanced type was essential to the survival of the Soviet Republic, and it had to be developed rapidly. Lenin had an enormous respect for the demonstrated abilities of American capitalists to organize large-scale production and expand it at a forced pace. He had no reason to believe that Rutgers, Haywood and Calvert had any such gifts. Certainly they had no such experience. Haywood and Calvert had been formed in a struggle in an advanced country to take over a production system of magnificent capacity. That offered no assurances that they could solve the problem of building up production in Siberia, where development was still at a primitive stage.

Lenin's superior grasp of the problems of industrial development enabled him to see the weaknesses in the leadership and in the principles of the project as proposed and so ardently advocated by the other three. They were totally possessed by their idea of an exclusive reliance on experienced workingclass militants and salaried engineers from countries where advanced production had already been achieved. In this enthusiastic workingclass internationalism there was a strong element of romanticism. In their feverish intoxication the three proponents were neglecting to consider the enormous difficulties in building industry in backward Russia with human material recruited in the United States.

Nothing came of Lenin's proposal to "improve the composition of the group by including say, four American businessmen". It is not clear whether Martens discussed it either with Hammer or with Rutgers. It would have been a surprising marriage but perhaps a fruitful one.

Julius Hammer's offer to deliver one million poods of wheat was accepted by the Soviet Government and on November 1, 1921, his company, the American Amalgamated Drug and Chemical Corporation, received a concession for working asbestos mines in the Alapaevsk District in the Urals. This was the first concession agreement concluded with a foreign capitalist company and gave Lenin great satisfaction. He was looking for a "path leading to the American business world." (He reiterated this several months later in a message to Stalin, on May 24, 1922 [ibid. 586]).

Final agreement

Negotiations with the Rutgers group continued without intrusion from American businessmen. Lenin had some doubts about underwriting the project, expressed in a letter of October 12,

1921, to the Politburo. There he summarized the arguments pro and con:

A difficult question:

For: if the Americans keep their word, it will be of tremendous benefit. In that case we shall not grudge 600,000 gold rubles.

Against: will they keep their word? Haywood is half-anarchist. More sentimental than business-like. Rutgers may succumb to Leftism. Calvert is highly garrulous. We have no business guarantees whatever. Enthusiastic people, in an atmosphere of unemployment, may recruit a group of "adventurous spirits" who will end up in squabbles. We may then lose part of our 600,000 gold rubles (they will, of course, spoil and waste some of the property) and risk losing up to 1 million gold rubles more, because under Section 8 (the end of it) we undertake
"to reimburse the equivalent of expenditures on machines and tools brought in by the said emigrant".

No small risk.

For: Smirnov I. N. and Maximov (of the Urals) are local people, and they are for it.

Against: Martens should know the Americans well, and he is against.

Lenin

(Lenin, *C. W.* 42: 349).

On October 17th the Council of Labor and Defense gave formal approval to Lenin's proposal that the Rutgers–Calvert–Haywood project be rejected with the expression of hope that it be corrected by enlarging the group of initiators and clearly limiting the Soviet Government financial obligation to $300,000.

Calvert describes what happened next in a manuscript he compiled in 1970:

All members of our group wanted to work out agreement specifications that were satisfactory to the Soviet Union. All of us admired Lenin and were in favor of any changes suggested by him. Rutgers notified Lenin and the Council of Labor and Defense that we approved all provisions suggested.

Lenin had received this reply by October 19th. On that date he wrote to Martens that he thought "this reply of Rutgers's leads to a *positive decision of the whole business.*" He also wrote to V. M. Mikhailov, secretary of the Central Committee (C.C.) of the Bolshevik Party:

October 19, 1921

Comrade Mikhailov,

I enclose the reply of the Rutgers group to the C.L.D. decision (i.e., the C.C. resolution).

I think this is tantamount to an *acceptance* of our terms.

I enclose, therefore, a draft *C.C. resolution* and request you to *circulate* it among the Politbureau members *right away.* This is very urgent.

With communist greetings,

Lenin

(Lenin on U.S., 1970, 562).

The proposed decree that was enclosed in this letter provided that the agreement with the group "shall be deemed concluded." The Presidium of the Supreme Economic Council "shall within two days work out the final text of the amended contract to be submitted for the approval of the C.L.D." It further provided some conditions that were to be incorporated in the amended contract:

1) The C.L.D. must have a right to participate in the selection of additional candidates to the Organizing Committee (This would give Lenin and Martens the right to make nominations. Perhaps Lenin was still considering the possibility of nominating some American businessmen). Further, the final list must be subject to C.L.D. approval. (This would give C.L.D. a veto over an unsatisfactory panel).

2) The total financial commitment of the Soviet Government was to be limited to $300,000.

3) In the event the contract was annulled, financial obligations would be determined by a Soviet court or the Central Executive Committee of the Soviet Republic (ibid. 563).

The Politbureau of the Central Committee approved this decree on October 20, 1921.

The amendments to the contract were speedily prepared and on October 21, 1921, the Agreement in its final form was signed. On the side of the Soviet Republic, Pyotr Alekseevich Bogdanov, chairman of the Supreme Economic Council and member of the Council of People's Commissars, signed for the Council of Labor and Defense. The other party was called "an initiatory group of American Workmen". It now numbered five, all of whom signed: Haywood, Rutgers, Calvert, Beyer and Barker. The text of this Agreement is reproduced in Appendix A.

The crucial article dealing with enlargement of the Organizing Committee provided as follows:

> The Managing Board of the Colony shall be composed of Comrades already enumerated at the beginning of this agreement (Haywood, Rutgers, Calvert, Beyer, and Barker) and nine additional comrades representing various labor organizations of America and England, in agreement with the persons signing this agreement with C.L.D. and with final approval of the additional members by C.L.D.; the Council of Labor and Defense (C.L.D.) shall have a representative in the Managing Board of the Colony.

The possibility of naming businessmen to the Board seemed to have been foreclosed by this wording. The phrase employed, "nine additional comrades representing various labor organizations of America and England," expressed the philosophy of the "initiatory group" that the enterprise should be governed purely by workers. It is probable that Lenin's suggestion to Martens about businessmen received no serious consideration, if, indeed, it was brought up at all. Calvert does not mention it.

The Communist Rutgers had some cause to feel alien on this initial board with four IWW militants. But Rutgers knew them all to be committed to a broad participation by others than the IWW.

3

ORGANIZING AN AMERICAN COMMITTEE

The successful conclusion to the negotiations between the initiatory group (led by Rutgers and Calvert) and the Council of Labor and Defense (led by Lenin) brought on immediately the practical question: How was it to be implemented? The five members of the initiatory group gathered at the Hotel Lux to reach concrete decisions as to what the assignment and responsibility of each was to be. Tom Mann and Nat Watkins, British labor leaders, also attended this session.

In the eyes of Lenin, Rutgers was the best known element and the most trustworthy. This special trust made Rutgers the recipient of Soviet funds which would be needed to sustain the members of the group in their travel and work on behalf of the project they were about to implement. From the beginning Rutgers had a dominant leadership role in the group, based on his relationship to Lenin. On Rutgers's request supported by Lenin, the Council of Labor and Defense gave Rutgers on October 24, 1921, a right to veto any candidate proposed for the expanded Managing Board (Trincher 1967, 107). In effect, Rutgers took on a special responsibility to the Soviet authorities to see that their funds were well spent. They looked to him to exercise a critical surveillance over the others and to render an accounting on demand as to the funds expended and results achieved.

In working out specific assignments, certain questions were already predetermined. Haywood could not return to the United

States, nor could Beyer. Both had to expect a long period of incarceration in the U.S. with time added as punishment for their departure from the country in violation of bail conditions. Who, then, would go to the United States to establish an American recruiting office? And who would seek out "the nine additional comrades representing various labor organizations" called for by the Agreement with the Soviet Government to enlarge the Managing Board? Calvert's imaginative role in creating the idea of an industrial colony and getting it to Lenin's attention gave him a claim on the American assignment. In fact, he was the only other American in the founding five. His selection had been foretold by the passage in Rutgers's letter of September 12, 1921, which stated, "Calvert has the complete confidence of Haywood and myself". That letter had also suggested that Calvert be entrusted to form a committee "to organize in America, in co-operation with the general immigration committee, the necessary labor and directing forces and to purchase the necessary implements and materials." Now that the agreement was concluded, the U.S. assignment automatically fell to Calvert.

This was a fateful decision. Calvert was virtually unknown outside the IWW unions in Detroit and Chicago. He had not been tested in organizational tasks of broad scope. The impression he created is suggested by the phrase commonly used to describe him: "a wandering wobbly". There was affection in it but little suggestion of respect for the solid strength of a leader. He would need character and the wisdom of Solomon to resolve the innumerable problems bound to arise in the United States around such a novel and controversial project at such a complex historical moment. It is said that fools rush in where angels fear to tread. Here was a case where perhaps only a fool would have dared rush in. One thing Calvert did not lack was self-confidence.

To assist Calvert, the English-born IWW newspaper editor and labor organizer, Tom Barker, would accompany him to the United States. Barker had experience in Australia, New Zealand and South America but none in the United States.

Calvert's credential, signed by the other six members of this "Organization Committee," was printed on a piece of white silk handkerchief. It stated that the Organization Committee "instructs H. S. Calvert to go to America as Organizer for the Colony. He is to return in the spring of 1922 to Russia with American workers and experts. All Comrades and Fellow Workers are requested to assist him in his activity" (From unpublished 1970 manuscript by H. S. Calvert, now in the Kennell Collection). It is evident from this "instruction" that Calvert was to return to Russia in the spring of 1922. Apparently, the expectation of the committee then was that Calvert would take up residence at Kemerovo as a member of the Managing Board. In fact, events took quite a different course, as we shall see.

Jack Beyer took on the assignment of directing preparatory activities at Kemerovo during the winter of 1921–1922. The recently negotiated agreement obligated the Managing Board to provide from America "2,800 thoroughly skilled workers and a technical staff requisite for the Kuznetsk Basin." An additional "3,000 men" were to be provided for the Nadezhdinsk Works in the Urals. It seems to have been assumed from the beginning that family members could accompany workers and technical staff, so preparations would have to be made to house and accommodate a very large number of people. No timetable was worked out except that shipment of personnel and material was to begin in the spring of 1922. This assignment expressed a great deal of confidence in Beyer.

Bill Haywood's assignment was to remain in Moscow. As between Rutgers and Haywood, there is no question that Rutgers was by far the more effective mover and shaker of the Soviet structure. He had many contacts in the government, a fair knowledge of Russian and the prestige of his participation in the founding of the Communist International. It was very unfortunate that those assets were not being exploited during the crucial early months of 1922 in Moscow. Rutgers's assignment was to go to the Netherlands and serve as liaison between Moscow and New York. There he would be able to rejoin his family, and undoubtedly that was a strong attraction. The result was that he was away from the two principal scenes of action, Moscow and New York, for six months while events were taking place that altered the destiny of Kuzbas. He might well have given those events a different shape had he stayed in Moscow to assist Haywood or gone to New York to assist Calvert and Barker. (Whether he could have gained admission into the United States at that time is a question.) It seems fair to say in the wisdom of hindsight that all the members of the Organizing Committee were carried away by their success in negotiating the agreement with the CLD and failed to do all that might have been done to protect it from the many doubters and opponents in both countries who were bound to create obstacles, especially in the early stages of implementation.

Rutgers's surrogate

Calvert and Barker left Moscow for the United States in the latter part of November, 1921. Rutgers was already beginning to have doubts about Calvert's ability to handle the assignment. A passage from Sebald Rutgers's biography written by his daughter and based on his statements to her from his recollections gives an insight into Rutgers's state of mind:

> Calvert was to go [to the United States]. Calvert cut deep wrinkles on Sebald's forehead. No, this was not distrust. Calvert was sincerely enthused with the Kuzbas idea. He wanted to work. Sebald knew very well how he was able to exaggerate—to be carried away with his own thoughts, with little ability to understand people (Trincher 1967, 106).

This explains why Rutgers wrote to Julius Heiman in New York asking him to keep a close eye on Calvert's performance and report to Rutgers. Heiman had been Rutgers's comrade in the League of Socialist Propaganda, and Rutgers judged him to be "wise, honest, sober and businesslike." He was to give Calvert "timely and shrewd advice", and he was to warn Rutgers of difficulties if they arose. Calvert was informed that Heiman would be reporting to Rutgers and that Heiman would be speaking *for* Rutgers. The arrangement, never veiled from Calvert, was seen by Rutgers as a way of strengthening the American committee for its tasks. It also revealed the change that was developing in Rutgers's attitude toward Calvert. It was clear that Calvert no longer enjoyed Rutgers's "complete confidence". Assuming that Rutgers was expressing his true judgment on September 12, 1921, when he used that phrase of support for Calvert in his letter to Lenin, the intervening months of close association and collaboration in the Moscow negotiations had modified his opinion.

In the interview with Lenin on September 19, 1921 Calvert had laid stress on his membership in and support of the IWW. According to Calvert's account, Lenin had said:

> I have every confidence in the IWW, a revolutionary proletarian group. Here in Russia, such groups have joined with the Bolsheviks in building the Soviet government.

But Lenin had also indicated the importance of recruiting workers other than IWW members to serve in the projected colony. As recollected by Calvert this exchange took place:

> *Calvert:* I don't think we will have any difficulty in bringing in all the different groups. I don't think it's going to be exclusively an IWW organization.
> *Lenin:* I'm glad to hear you say that. We want it inclusive.
> (From taped recollections of Calvert in possession of his widow, Rachel Calvert).

We have already learned that Rutgers shared Lenin's view that the recruiting effort should reach outside the IWW, although he anticipated that most of the workers would come from its ranks. In the hope that Calvert could gain the support of American Communists for the Kuzbas project, Rutgers gave him a list of several names, members of the Communist Party of the United States, who were to be approached with an invitation to join the American Organization Committee. Among these names were: Ludwig Lore, James Cannon, Matt Mulari and Edgar Owens (from an unpublished manuscript, "The American Organization Committee Kuzbas" by Mellie Calvert; Kennell Collection).

Problems with leaders of the IWW

It was the misfortune of Calvert and Barker that they chanced to arrive in the United States precisely at a moment when the new leadership of the IWW in Chicago was publicly denouncing the Communist International, the Soviet government and the Communist Party (Bolshevik) led by Lenin. This fierce polemic grew out of the proceedings at the RILU Congress in Moscow as reported and interpreted by an IWW delegate, George Williams. The General Executive Board of the IWW made bitter anti-Soviet recommendations on December 10, 1921, on the basis of the Williams report. Calvert and Barker suddenly found themselves at the center of a political storm. It greatly affected the environment in which they were to work. We must explore this controversy, because it influenced the history of Kuzbas.

The IWW had established a reputation as a militant organization of workers aiming at the overthrow of capitalism. It was this proletarian revolutionary goal that evoked Lenin's goodwill and his cordial salutes to the IWW. (The IWW General Executive Board had formally endorsed the Communist International in 1920 [Foster, 1952, 182].) Undoubtedly with Lenin's approval, the IWW was invited to attend the founding international congress of "Red Trade Unions" (RILU). It was this Congress that provided the occasion for Calvert to go to Moscow in the spring of 1921 as a delegate from the Detroit chapter of the IWW.

The IWW had long followed the principle of fighting the reformist leadership of the American Federation of Labor by establishing separate unions, organized along industrial lines, and competing with the AF of L unions for members. This was the principle of "dual unions" or "parallel unions" that came under severe attack by Lenin in his pamphlet, *Left Wing Communism*. Lenin argued that proletarian revolutionaries should join the reformist unions because these provided the best access to daily contact with large masses of workers.

Some in the IWW leadership were also troubled by another aspect of Bolshevik policy. This related to the question of the dictatorship of the proletariat. Lenin's writings and Bolshevik policy were making clear one aspect of this concept: the proletarian dictatorship was to be administered through a proletarian *state* power. Labor unions were not to be completely autonomous; they were not to be completely independent of the Communist Party, which had the broader responsibility to guide and coordinate the unions in a government of the whole class. To many from the IWW (among them Haywood, Beyer and Calvert) this seemed no cause for denouncing the Bolsheviks. But to the new post-Haywood leadership of the IWW, this was contrary to a fundamental IWW principle, syndicalism, the sovereign authority of the union. Therefore, when the invitation to participate in an international "Red Trade Union" congress in Moscow arrived, it posed a problem to the IWW leaders. They decided to accept, but as the *only* authorized delegate they named George Williams, with instructions to stand firm on all issues dividing syndicalists from Bolsheviks. (Calvert had gone from Detroit without authorization from the national office).

Syndicalists from various countries gathered in Berlin prior to the Moscow congress and there drew up a syndicalist manifesto. Among the signers were George Williams and Tom Barker. This demanded an "independent economic international." By "independent" was meant politically independent of the policies of the Communist International and the Communist Party of Lenin, the Bolsheviks.

At the RILU Congress, the syndicalists were in a minority and saw themselves voted down on all these issues. The Congress consolidated the leading position of Leninist policies in the RILU. The newly-elected General Secretary, A. Lozovsky, was also a member of the Central Committee of the Russian Communist Party (Bolshevik).[6]

On dual unionism, the following "Resolution on Questions of Tactics" was approved by the Congress over the objections of Williams and other syndicalists:

> The IWW, an independent organization in America, is too weak to take the place of the old labor unions. The IWW have a purely anarchistic prejudice against politics and political action, being divided into supporters and opponents of such a cardinal question as proletarian dictatorship . . . . Therefore the question of creating revolutionary cells and groups inside the American Federation of Labor is of vital importance. There is no other way by which one could gain the working mass in America than to lead a systematic struggle within the unions. (The First Congress of the Red Trades Union International at Moscow, 1921: A Report of the Proceedings by George Williams, Delegate from the IWW." Published by IWW, Chicago, Illinois, 1921).

When Williams returned to the United States from Moscow he launched a campaign within the IWW to turn the organization against participation in the RILU and against cooperation with the Communist International. In the report cited above, he further charged that

> . . . . the political faction [i.e. the Communists] did not want an economic international in fact but in name only . . . a real international of revolutionary industrial unions would become such a powerful organization . . . that the political organizations would have to surrender their present dominating position. The tacticians in the Communist International know this, therefore they are making every effort to control such an organization and keep it in the embryo stage . . . I am convinced that

a truly economic international of revolutionary industrial unions cannot exist with headquarters in Moscow without being dominated by the Communist International.

Williams also wrote that "the Communists" want "liquidation of the revolutionary labor organizations into the conservative labor bodies of the various countries".

Having distributed the Williams Report, the General Executive Board of the IWW (Robert E. Daly, Chairman; John Grady, General Secretary) then issued the statement that exacerbated the difficulties facing Calvert and Barker. It recommended that the IWW not affiliate in any manner with the RILU. Finally and most important, "the IWW would find it impossible to cooperate with the Communist Party of America" (GEB of IWW, Statement of December 10, 1921).

It was the fate of Calvert and Barker to be knocking at the doors of the IWW leadership while that statement was being drafted. They had gone to Chicago immediately on arrival in the United States, bearing their copy of the Kuzbas Agreement and expecting to evoke with it as much excitement in the IWW main office as they themselves felt. Instead, the reception was a cold bath of hostility. It did no good to cite the support of the great Lenin. He was a principal source of the Bolshevik policies that were under attack in the Chicago headquarters. Calvert and Barker were told that they would receive no official support from the IWW and that the Kuzbas project could not be advertised and promoted in IWW publications.

Haywood's membership in the Communist Party, his residence in Moscow, and his presence at the RILU Congress, which might have reassured this new IWW General Executive Board, were rather grounds for opposition to anything he promoted. To them, Haywood was no longer the honored founder of the IWW. He was the traitor who had left his bondsmen to pay the consequences. Beyer was tarred with the same brush.

Another cool reception

Calvert and Barker had been joined in Chicago by Calvert's wife, Mellie, who withdrew from her classes at the University of California when Calvert told her by telephone there was a role for her in the new enterprise. Disappointed, of course, by what had taken place at the IWW, the three boarded a train for New York hoping they would have better luck with the Communists they were to seek out and invite to join the Organizing Committee.

According to Mellie Calvert's unpublished manuscript on "The American Organizing Committee", Calvert and Barker experienced more cold baths in New York. She wrote:

> First of all Barker and Cal called on Ludwig Lore and found that he was so busy with his own work he could not even attend Kuzbas committee meetings.
>
> Next they went to see James Cannon and I tagged along. He was a high Communist Party official and we met him at the Party headquarters in New York. With him was another high Communist official, Charles Ruthenberg. We found that they refused to serve on the Organization Committee, or to give the Kuzbas project the official backing of the Communist Party.

In this first meeting with Cannon and Ruthenberg, Mellie Calvert formed the impression that Communist Party support for Kuzbas was blocked by considerations other than the following stated ones:

1) Participation by the Party would subject the Kuzbas organization to harassment by the police.

2) The Communist Party should not endanger its reputation by supporting an enterprise that might prove a failure.

To Calvert and Barker, those were hardly adequate reasons for refusal to support a project recommended by Lenin. They pressed hard with the point of Lenin's involvement, and this finally produced some effect: Cannon agreed to attend a meeting to discuss organization of an American committee.

Calvert and Barker then contacted two other Communists on Rutgers's list, Matti Mulari and Edgar Owens. They agreed to help.

Julius Heiman had received letters from Rutgers and was willing and ready to participate as Rutgers's representative.

The first meeting of prospective members of the American Organization Committee Kuzbas was held on January 2, 1922. Present were: H. Calvert, Barker, Cannon, Mulari, Owens and Heiman. Mellie Calvert was also present as secretary, and she recorded the minutes.

Heiman requested that each nominee to the Committee give his reasons for accepting or rejecting the nomination. Cannon stated that he declined the nomination because his participation would officially involve the Communist Party. A committee of the Party, he said, had decided that the Party would not in any way interfere with the work of the Organization Committee; but neither would the Party as such take a position in support of the project. According to Mellie, "Calvert asked if the Communist press would accept Kuzbas publicity and Cannon said no." Cannon said the hostile attitude of the General Executive Board of the IWW "had put the Party on its guard". The Party intended to take a public position in support of the RILU. "There will be a bitter struggle" over this with the IWW. Cannon said he doubted the wisdom of sending men to Russia who are "identified with an organization that is against Soviet Russia".

Calvert and Barker brought forth all the arguments that had proved effective in Moscow in winning approval by the Council of Labor and Defense (which of course implied approval by the Bolshevik Party). These did not sway Cannon. According to Mellie, Calvert indicated to Cannon that the Communist Party could have a dominant position in the Organization Committee "to take the Kuzbas concession and handle it" (Rutgers would undoubtedly have approved such a structure). At the very least, Calvert argued, the Party should give "moral support to other revolutionists who were willing to go ahead with the job".

It is idle to speculate over what might have been. The fact is that the young Communist Party, preoccupied with severe government repression and its own consolidation,[7] declined to take the reins from Calvert and Barker in promoting Kuzbas among left-wing workers and a broader public of the progressive-minded who were also looking for a way to provide international support to the new workers' state. "Cannon stated that his time was taken up with other work". The inference is very strong that Cannon regarded Calvert and Barker with a good deal of skepticism. Unfortunately, they were virtual unknowns on the New York scene, and their claims to support from Lenin were not weighty enough to overcome the divisive effects of the attacks on the Party coming out of the Chicago IWW headquarters.

The meeting was not a total loss. Mulari and Owens agreed to join Calvert and Barker on the Organization Committee. Matti Mulari was an auto mechanic well-known and respected among

Finnish immigrant workers. Edgar Owens had experience and standing from his work on a Labor Defense Committee. Both were members of the Communist Party.

But that was small consolation for the two major setbacks received and the third which followed a few days later. The Society for Technical Aid to Russia advised Calvert and Barker that it, too, would provide no publicity and no material or moral support to the new organization. What reasons were given we do not know.

Julius Heiman wrote Rutgers that creation of the Kuzbas committee did not seem possible in such a negative atmosphere. Rutgers formed an opinion that "Calvert and Barker under present conditions are not the proper persons to get a strong organization committee together." (Rutgers's letter of February 25, 1922, as quoted by Mellie Calvert).

It is to the great credit of Calvert and Barker that they did not despair under these disappointments. They sought opportunities to speak about Kuzbas at union meetings, to liberal groups and at ethnic community halls. They also pursued writers with access to the general public. The story they were proffering had a good charge of sensational value, and the result was that the news about the plan to create an American industrial colony in Siberia reached a nationwide audience. It is probable that Calvert the salesman drew heavily on his own enthusiasm in some of these interviews, painting a picture of the Kuznetsk Basin that was more romantic than realistic.

A feature writer for the New York *World*, Charles W. Wood, after spending several hours with Calvert, wrote a leading article for the Sunday edition of February 12, 1922, with Calvert's picture and the headline, "H. S. Calvert's Giant Task in Industry: Once a Worker in a Ford Factory He Has Engaged to Develop a Russian Territory Bigger Than New Jersey." Wood was excited by the magnitude of the project and conveyed this to his readers. Mike Gold wrote a long article for the March *Liberator* magazine entitled "Pioneers for Siberia". An article in *The Nation* magazine was read by thousands. Calvert, through interviews with Stuart Chase, Max Eastman, Thorstein Veblen and Roger Baldwin, gained support from writers and public figures with wide audiences. There was an abundance of publicity. The fact that Gold, Eastman and the *Liberator* were known to be close to the Communist Party strengthened with Party members and sympathizers the credibility of a project they had embraced. The Party made no overt attempt to discourage volunteers.

A prospectus

Calvert and Barker rented an office at 110 West 40th Street in New York City. Mellie Calvert took on duties as secretary. Inquiries began to pour in, evoked by the spreading waves of publicity. Some ready form of prospectus was needed to answer the standard questions and encourage applications. Calvert and Barker spent several days in its preparation. It was a booklet of 32 pages, well organized and clearly written, entitled *Kuzbas: An Opportunity For Workers and Engineers*. It became a principal recruiting tool. In the introductory section the spirit of the project was described in the following words:

> Every worker should read the following pages carefully. In this pamphlet he will find all the details of a great plan whereby American workers and engineers can go to Russia, take over an immense industrial project, and develop it for the benefit of humanity. . . He will find a plan that will stimulate the imagination of men of industrial vision, a plan for the first industrial colony in the world where engineers will find freedom to work out experiments they cannot attempt under the profit system, and where workers will find that self-government, that sense of social creativeness, that solidarity and equality they have never found anywhere in the history of the world until this present hour.

Then followed a description of the desperate condition of the Russian economy, the birth of the Kuzbas idea in Moscow and a brief account of the survey expedition to the Kuznetsk Basin. Several pages were devoted to a detailed description of the natural resources and the existing industrial facilities in Kemerovo, Nadezhdinsk Works and Tomsk. Facts were presented for estimating the enormous potential of agricultural and industrial development in Siberia. "The possibilities of scientific machine agriculture are unlimited. Siberia has a great future, which only waits for the men who know how to realize on its possibilities".

There was a description of the climate in the Kuznetsk Basin:

> Kuznetsk Basin is just on the opposite side of the globe from Winnipeg, Canada, in the same latitude, and has generally the same climatic conditions. The average January temperature is zero Fahrenheit. . .

The winters are very cold, but dry. The first snow comes the first of October and is soon followed by winter. The snowfall during October is followed by bright sunny days all winter long. . . The summers are delightful with the greenest possible meadows.

The Prospectus advised that 25,000 acres of land had been assigned to the Colony:

A big machine farm will be organized. . . Steam and gas tractors, gang plows, threshers and mowers will be bought in America and taken with the unit. Two thousand head of dairy cattle and bulls, 500 head of horses, bees, swine, geese and ducks will be supplied by the Siberian Revolutionary Committee. . . The farm will organize a modern truck garden. This farm should interest the best American farmers and be not only a producer of food but a model of scientific agriculture.

The different categories of needed workers were listed: miners, farm workers, lumberjacks and general construction workers were the biggest categories, but there was also a need for doctors, dentists and teachers as well as "cooks, bakers, waiters, laundrymen, tailors, etc. necessary to maintain such efficient social standards as would result in average American efficiency for the enterprises". As for wives and children, as many as twelve hundred could be accommodated at Kemerovo and fifteen hundred at Nadezhdinsk. "The engineers and skilled workers will in many cases be accompanied by their families. . . Suitable schools will be provided for the children, and work in the homes or industrial work provided for the women. Single women will also be considered, providing they are also industrially qualified, physically fit and politically reliable." (Clearly, the drafters of the prospectus were not so anxious to receive applications from single women.)

In a paragraph headed "Wages" the authors wrote that "workers will receive from their production a satisfactory standard of living which will include a yearly bonus". What this meant specifically was not spelled out. No one was being promised high wages. "What is meant by a satisfactory standard of living will be determined by the board of managers, who are responsible both to the workers and to the Soviet Government". The amount of the yearly bonus would depend on production, hardships endured and the future prospects of Kuzbas.

Each worker who applied would be expected to supply "capital" in the amount of $300. Small tools could satisfy up to $100 of that obligation. The other $200 per worker would be used to buy transportation and a supply of food to be shipped to the Colony from the United States.

In fulfillment of a commitment made to Lenin by the initiatory group in Moscow, each applicant was required to sign a statement indicating that he had read and understood and that he accepted certain conditions. These were contained in extracts taken from the Organization Statute drafted in Moscow and in the four articles of the "Lenin Pledge". (See page 62). Some of the conditions related to government of the Colony. A crucial article provided:

> The management of the Unit will be in the hands of a Managing Board of seven members, three to reside in Kuzbas, three in the Urals and one in Moscow. These members will be selected by the workers in the Unit, subject to the approval of the Soviet authorities. The election will be for a term of one year, with the provision of recall by two-thirds of the workers, or by the Soviet Government, who will have a representative on the Managing Board.

This paragraph, which expressed the substance and the limits of the Colony's "autonomy", would later become a focus of controversy. Note also that the third of four articles in the Lenin Pledge provided as follows:

> The members of the Unit pledge themselves, in case of misunderstanding or conflict, that they will accept as final the decision of the highest Soviet authority in Russia.

The Prospectus effectively conveyed in its many pages the enthusiasm of the initiators of Kuzbas for their brainchild. It also carried on its final page a brief warning of the many privations that are unavoidably connected with the reconstruction of industry in a rather backward country (Article One of the Lenin Pledge). This imbalance was later blamed for having generated excessive expectations among potential volunteers. But, after all, it was drafted for use as a recruiting aid, and who can blame the authors for having accented the positive?

A committee is formed

The problem of creating an American Organization Committee had to be resolved in some manner or other. Mulari and Owens were helpful in finding a third Communist who consented to accept membership on the Committee. This was P. Pascal Cosgrove, a giant-sized Irishman with long experience as an organizer of the Shoemakers Union. Claire Killen, an electrician, made the third IWW member on the Committee, along with Calvert and Barker. After consultations with Heiman and Rutgers, it was decided to fill the other three places on the Committee with persons not connected with either the Communist Party or the IWW. They were usually referred to as "the liberals" on the Committee. The best known among them was attorney Roger Baldwin, founder and President of the American Civil Liberties Union. A second was Mont Schuyler, a management engineer whom Calvert met and recruited through the New York *World* writer, Charles Wood. The third "liberal" member of the Committee was Thomas Reese, a sheet and tin plate worker from Granite City, Illinois.

These nine met for the first time as the American Organization Committee on March 3, 1922. Rutgers had expressed a hope that some well-known Communist would act as Chairman of the Committee. It was still the expectation that Calvert would be accompanying the first group of colonists to the Soviet Republic, as stated in his "credential". Mellie Calvert reports in her manuscript that no Communist would accept the chair of the Committee, despite further urging by Heiman and Calvert. That was a disappointing reality to which Rutgers had to adjust. In this situation the Committee elected Calvert the Chairman, and he accepted. It was clear that Rutgers was not happy with this outcome. He wrote that neither Calvert nor Barker should pass on Kuzbas applicants. He feared they would be biased in favor of IWW members and sympathizers, whereas Rutgers wanted to do everything possible to increase Communist participation. Calvert and Barker agreed to leave the decision on selection of applicants to others.

Mont Schuyler, the management engineer, soon emerged as a strong believer in the promise of the enterprise and one of the most active members of the Committee. He became manager of the New York office, thereby freeing Calvert and Barker for their recruiting trips to cities in different parts of the country. Schuyler won the respect of Mellie Calvert, who worked as his secretary. Here is her appraisal:

He [Schuyler] was a trained efficiency engineer. He was so intelligent, efficient and knowledgeable that anything he touched was quickly and well done. Although he was not affiliated with any radical organization, he saw the magnitude and importance of Kuzbas, and was just as enthusiastic and self-sacrificing as anyone else in the office.

Cosgrove and Mulari also worked full time in the New York office, receiving subsistence compensation, as did Schuyler, Calvert and Barker. They were paid from Soviet funds sent to the Committee from time to time by Rutgers. The other four members of the Committee served as volunteers on an irregular basis as their time permitted. In March, 1922, as inquiries and applications began to come in, the office employed a second secretary, Lucille Strawn, to assist Mellie Calvert. Barker, who had a penchant for writing, handled most of the correspondence. Herbert Calvert was frequently on the road.

Recruiting colonists

Matt Mulari became a one-man department in charge of recruiting and passing on the applications of Finns. He used the Finnish press and Finnish community groups as media for publicity. Finnish colonists awaiting transportation in New York were under his care. He had selected them, and he made an effort to prepare them carefully for their new life. They were an important part of the recruits sent to Siberia in 1922 (approximately thirty percent).

Other applications were reviewed and either approved or disapproved by Cosgrove, a Communist, and Schuyler, a non-party engineer. The Committee at its first meeting on March 3rd formally adopted a policy of approving applications "on a nonpartisan basis". By this was meant there would be no quotas or restrictions relating to party affiliation. Since Calvert was making use of his IWW credentials and ideology in publicizing the project, it appealed to many IWW sympathizers as an opportunity to implement their theories on building and managing industry under worker control. Calvert undoubtedly shared this vision with many of the workers he recruited. The selection committee (though it included no IWW representative) carried out its nonpartisan mandate and rejected no one simply for political reasons. The result was that a heavy component of IWW members and sympathizers applied and were accepted.

The fact that the colony was to be established in Siberia and would help build industry for the new Soviet Republic made it attractive to Communists. So they, too, applied in substantial numbers.

Thus it was that at a time of great friction between the leaders of the IWW and the Communist Party, Kuzbas recruiting went forward in such a way as to bring together in distant Kemerovo Colony contingents of strongly partisan members and sympathizers from these two groups, who probably would have elected to avoid each other had they stayed in the United States. A setting for internal conflict was being created. We shall examine in later chapters how this potential for antagonism worked itself out.

A special effort was required to recruit the qualified engineers who would be needed to give technical direction in Kemerovo and in the Urals. In this Calvert had assistance from Charles W. Wood and Mont Schuyler. Charles Steinmetz, an outstanding electrical engineer employed by the General Electric Company, immediately became interested in helping Calvert recruit. It was in February, 1922, that Steinmetz expressed in a letter to Lenin his "admiration of the wonderful work of social and industrial regeneration which Russia is accomplishing under such terrible difficulties" (*Lenin on U.S.*, 641). From Steinmetz's first contact with the Kuzbas enterprise until his death in October, 1923, he was an outspoken advocate for its recognition and success. Other engineers who showed support by advertising the project favorably in engineering communities were Walter Polakov, Howard Scott and C. A. Mekler, the latter a metallurgical engineer who helped organize a Kuzbas recruiting and fundraising group in Chicago.

Calvert had authority to negotiate special contract terms with experienced engineers in order to induce them to accept posts in Siberia or the Urals. He used this to recruit William Van Hoffen, a steel engineer with U.S. Steel Corporation in Gary, Indiana, for assignment at Nadezhdinsk Works, and Dr. William H. Mahler, a chemical engineer, to direct the completion of the chemical factory in Kemerovo. The third major technical post would be direction of the mines at Kemerovo. For this assignment Calvert recruited Alfred Pearson, Jr., chief engineer of the Pennsylvania May Coal Company. Several other engineers of lesser status and practical experience also signed up, some from political conviction, some in search of further experience. Among these, we can identify by name:

Walter H. Popp, mechanical engineer from Buffalo, New York.

Benjamin Steinhardt, chemical engineer who became Mahler's assistant.

Harry Ostroll, who became assistant to Van Hoffen.

Noah Lerner, electrical engineer.

Carl Sundbach, engineer from Boston.

Leonard A. White, mechanical engineer from Alaska.

Samuel Shipman, management engineer, graduate of Cornell University.

First groups depart

At the end of March, 1922, a group of 60 men and 8 women, one with a three-month-old baby, assembled in New York City to prepare for departure as the first contingent of Kuzbas pioneers. They sailed on April 8, 1922, aboard the S.S. *Adriatic*. Only Engineer Van Hoffen and his secretary had cabin accommodations. The rest were in steerage. Dr. Mahler was entrusted with $1,500 by the Organization Committee to cover expenses of the group enroute. Each worker and engineer took his own tools and equipment for use at his new job. Another 38 tons of cargo, mostly food supplies and equipment purchased by the Organization Committee, also accompanied the group. Dr. Mahler, assisted by a Communist, Benjamin Steinhardt, acted as general coordinator during the journey. The group debarked at Liverpool and traveled by train with their cargo to Hull, where they boarded another vessel bound for Latvia. At Libau (Liepaja) they again debarked and traveled by train to Riga and thence to the border with Russia. The reception there was cordial as soon as Dr. Mahler displayed credentials from the American Organization Committee and explained the group's purpose and destination.

The hardship of travel in Russia was soon brought home. The trip to Moscow, which lasted three days, had to be made in boxcars. They pulled into a freight yard and found no one to receive them. Russian railroad officials housed the group in an old, abandoned building while a search was made for Haywood. He had gone to Petrograd on the understanding that the group would arrive there. Bill Shatov, the representative of the Council of Labor and Defense on the Managing Board, conveyed a welcome from the Soviet Government. It was a happy coincidence that this first group of colonists had arrived in Moscow on the eve of May Day celebrations, so Shatov arranged for their attendance. The presence of the group stirred applause and excitement on a day filled with optimism and warm expressions of international solidarity!

Haywood arrived back in Moscow on May 2nd and with Shatov's assistance arranged further transportation to final destinations. Van Hoffen and his new bride (he and his secretary were wedded in Moscow) departed with four other men from the group to travel to the steel mills of Nadezhdinsk Works. The rest boarded third and fourth class railroad cars for a 2,400-mile journey east on the Trans–Siberian Railway across the vast steppes of Russia, across the Ural Mountains, thence across the lowlands of Siberia, through Omsk and Novo–Nikolaevsk to Yurga, where the two coaches and three boxcars of the colonists were detached from the Trans–Siberian train to await a train south into the Kuznetsk Basin.

The colonists had ample food supplies with them, some of which they traded along the way for local produce peddled at railroad stations. Dysentery found its way into the railroad cars of the colonists, making the three week journey from Moscow a miserable experience for about eighty percent of the group. They arrived in Kemerovo at the end of May, 1922, approximately seven weeks after their departure from New York. They had reason to be weary and worn and many were weak from the accursed dysentery, but all were filled with excitement mingled with apprehension as they entered the region and finally, at the end of the line where it reached the River Tom, the town that was to be their new home.

By the time the first group arrived at Kemerovo, a second group, numbering 101 persons, had sailed from New York (on May 13, 1922, on the S.S. *Rotterdam*). Calvert had given up his intention to accompany one of the early groups to Kemerovo. He had become an indefatigable recruiter and was playing a major role as Chairman of the Organization Committee. By staying in the United States, Calvert undoubtedly thought he was serving where he was most needed. He did not realize that developments were taking place in Moscow and in the mind of Rutgers that would undermine Calvert's place in the enterprise. He would have better served his own interest had he carried through with the original plan to establish himself as a leading figure in Kemerovo as the Colony was founded.

The Kuzbas Bulletin

Calvert in one of his promotional talks made a very favorable impression on a clergyman, William Montgomery Brown, D.D., whose book *Communism and Christianity* had caused the author to be removed from his office as Bishop of Arkansas and accused by some of heresy and by others of mental derangement. Dr. Brown made a gift of the proceeds from the sale of his book to the Kuzbas organization. He also made an immediate cash gift of $500 to enable the Organization Committee to commence publication of a bulletin reporting information about the enterprise.

Tom Barker was assigned the responsibility of editing what became known as the *Kuzbas Bulletin*. The first issue was dated May 20, 1922, and thereafter it appeared at intervals of approximately one month until it ceased publication in December, 1923. It carried a wide variety of information about the Kuzbas project, including job descriptions of workers needed, reports on recruitment activities and progress, letters from colonists describing their surroundings and experiences, pictures of groups preparing to depart from New York and reprints from Soviet publications about developments that would affect life in the Colony. Issues sold quickly at five cents a copy, and soon there was a subscription list long enough to make the publication self-sustaining.

The *Bulletin* became a medium through which the colonists and the Organization Committee could communicate their news and views about Colony problems and prospects to the general public. Rutgers and Haywood used it to publish their reports from time to time, documents which are now a valuable source of information on the course of the Colony's history.

In summing up the results achieved in 1922, it is clear that recruiting did not proceed at the pace envisaged when the agreement was signed in 1921. In fact, by August 26, 1922, the date of the departure of the fifth and final group that year from the United States, the total number of male workers and engineers had reached 302. Surely that total would have been higher had Calvert received the full backing of the leaders of the Communist Party, the Society for Technical Aid to Russia and the IWW.

How much he himself was to blame for their abstention is an open question. Mainly, he was the victim of a political conjuncture not of his making; it was short-lived, but it lasted long enough to embarrass all effort to create a stronger American Committee and tap the full resources of established organizations.

But those circumstantial and unforeseeable handicaps were probably not the principal cause for the striking deficit between the figures mentioned in Moscow in 1921 and the number actually recruited in 1922 and thereafter. Rutgers, Calvert and Haywood had overestimated the number of Americans willing and able promptly to volunteer for work in such an unprecedented project. The hardships of life in the Soviet Republic were notorious; the United States government was doing everything it could to harass leftwing militants and to depict the Soviet regime as a hopeless failure doomed to an early extinction. The will to defy such dissuasion was bound to be something of a rarity. Postwar employment was also on the upswing in the United States by 1922. There was more optimism than realism in the promises that emerged from the enthusiasm of the initiatory group.

Furthermore, there was no pressure from Rutgers or Moscow during 1922 to accelerate the real pace of recruitment. On the contrary, Rutgers concluded that it was going to be difficult to accommodate and absorb even a few hundred colonists, let alone several thousand. As we shall see, he and Haywood were urging Calvert to slow the pace of recruitment and reduce the flow. This too was a factor in the policy and the performance of the American Organization Committee.

4

ESTABLISHMENT
OF THE COLONY

Jack Beyer was a Seminole Indian and an artist whose main source of livelihood in the United States was painting signs. He had joined the IWW in its early years and thereafter made it the center of his life. Together with Haywood and the other principal IWW leaders he had been arrested on charges of "criminal syndicalism" for his opposition to the war and for his advocacy of a Workers Cooperative Republic which would "finally burst the shell of capitalist government." Like Haywood, Beyer had been found guilty in Judge Landis's court in Chicago in 1918. He, too, elected to save himself from the threat of a long jail sentence by leaving the United States for Moscow while free on bond pending a higher court's decision on his appeal from the conviction. In Moscow he had joined Haywood, Calvert and Rutgers in promoting the Kuzbas project among delegates to the RILU Congress. He was among the "initiatory group of American workmen" who signed the Agreement with the Soviet Republic on October 21, 1921.

In the division of responsibilities among the founders, it was Beyer's assignment to assist Haywood in recruiting workers, Americans or returning immigrants, who were already in Moscow. These were to be sent under Beyer's leadership to Kemerovo, where they would join Emil Feltman, the German-American miner, Charlie Maskalunas, interpreter and lumber worker, and the sixteen other American lumbermen who were already working with the Siberian Revolutionary Committee in cutting logs and moving them to Kemerovo. Haywood and Beyer recruited approximately another 15 workers, among them Charles Schwartz, Jack Harper and a rigger, Harry Sussman. Many of the recruits were Finns with experience as lumberjacks or carpenters in the United States and Canada. In the middle of winter they traveled from Moscow to Novo–Nikolaevsk, where Beyer established contact with the leaders of the Siberian Revolutionary Committee and received their support in planning and preparing the construction projects that would be needed to provide lodging in Kemerovo for later arrivals from the United States.

Beyer thus became the first director of the Autonomous Industrial Colony, dividing his time between Novo–Nikolaevsk and Kemerovo. It was a rugged task for a man in his 64th year, who spoke little Russian and had not much experience in construction. He suffered a blow and the project a loss in that winter of 1921–1922 when Charlie Maskalunas, the veteran Estonian worker and fighter for the October Revolution, contracted typhus and died.

One of Beyer's first acts was to join the Carpenters Union in Kemerovo. Beyer had the good sense to see that relations with the local people would be all-important to the fate of the colony. Despite the language barrier, Beyer established friendships with the workers of Kemerovo. Perhaps his own origins and life struggles helped him to win more easily the trust and confidence of these strangers who had also known oppression. They would now work together to help each other. It was exactly this kind of sympathy and mutual support on which the hopes of Kuzbas were founded.

These American pioneers, as they were being named in the United States, were not called upon to create a new base on an uninhabited frontier. They were moving into an established Siberian community of approximately ten thousand people. A coal mine was a going operation under the management of engineers and technicians who directed a work force of experienced miners and numerous administrative and clerical personnel. On the other bank, the left (west) bank of the Tom River, where the main body of the population of Kemerovo lived, a chemical factory had been under construction since 1916. This had been a project of a French and Belgian company designed to utilize coal as raw material in the production of coke and various chemical by-products. Hundreds of local residents were employed in the construction of the plant and in the handling of coal, which came across the river in buckets by cable either for use in Kemerovo or for loading aboard railroad cars and shipment to other destinations. Kemerovo was the railhead of a spur line that joined the railroad running north from Kuznetsk to a junction with the Trans–Siberian Railroad. It was thus a kind of regional transportation center with a certain amount of industrial activity. Calvert had called it "a little Gary, Indiana."

Each of these enterprises had its hierarchy of managers, technicians and workers, many of them experienced in their jobs and totally dependent on them for a livelihood. Naturally they were apprehensive at the news that Kemerovo had been chosen as the location for a colony of foreign workers and technicians, whose task it would be to reorganize production to make it more efficient. This was a threat to established practices, to the prestige and authority of the Russian experts (the *spetsy*), holdovers from the old regime, and even to the jobs of ordinary workmen. The enthusiasm of the Siberian Revolutionary Committee for the Kuzbas project was communicated to local Party organs and to trade union officials, but in the general population of Kemerovo there were bound to be reservations and even some hostility toward these disturbing intruders from the outside world.

Beyer relied on his class instincts to find the welcome he would need to begin his work. His decision to seek membership in the Carpenters Union was just the right gesture, expressing with his simple sincerity the desire of an American worker to join in the already existing worker organizations of Kemerovo as the framework of a new international solidarity. His application was accepted, and immediately Beyer had a local identity and local contacts which would prove invaluable in the months ahead.

The support of carpenters was especially important, because living quarters would have to be constructed for the foreign workers who had already arrived and for those others who would be arriving from the United States in a few months. Beyer was not an experienced carpenter, and even those among his forces who knew something of the craft lacked tools. Meetings in which Beyer brought together his fellow workers of different nationalities produced plans for the construction of a community house on the mine side (the right bank) of the Tom River. This would be large enough to house approximately two hundred workers. Local carpenters helped with the planning, the preparatory work and with the loan of tools.

The Kemerovo carpenters were, it seems, infected by the enthusiasm of this first contingent of American workers to enter their world. On February 8, 1922, the Carpenters Union of the Kemerovo Mining District passed the following resolution and had it published in a local newspaper:

> We, the members of the Carpenters Union greet the representatives of the American workers for their attention and proffered help to the Young Republic of Soviet Russia, and we hope that by our combined efforts we will be able to build up our destroyed industries; and by that method we will be able to guarantee our international revolutionary rights and thus aid the world proletariat to free themselves from the chains of capitalism.

That was an auspicious beginning. The editors of the Kuzbas Bulletin in the United States recognized the importance of this grass-roots resolution and published it verbatim in their first issue.

Blows to morale

During the spring of 1922, with no new construction sufficiently advanced for occupancy, Beyer and his team lived in a few log huts they found empty and in a dilapidated military barracks that had been occupied and then abandoned by a labor battalion detailed at some previous period to work in the mines. (During the civil war these same barracks had been occupied by the troops of Admiral Kolchak. The mine side of Kemerovo had been a White base.)

If Beyer was expected to have suitable living quarters ready and waiting for the first contingent of Americans, who sailed from New York on April 8, 1922, and arrived in Kemerovo seven weeks later, it is clear he did not perform that miracle. The housing shortage was aggravated by refugees from the famine and by the continued presence of draftees into the Labor Army.

In that first contingent to arrive in Kemerovo from the United States there were 55 men, seven women and a baby under six months old. This was the first striking evidence of a lack of coordination among the different directing centers of the international enterprise. At about one-month intervals the Organization

Committee based in New York sent over four more contingents in the summer of 1922, each of them including substantial numbers of women and children. Every new arrival added to the crisis of a housing shortage that was not to be solved more or less satisfactorily until the partially completed Community House could be opened to 150 occupants near the end of 1922. In the meantime many bitter words had been passed among the disappointed colonists, particularly those accompanied by their families. Some continued to dwell in the railroad coaches or boxcars in which they had traveled from Moscow; others moved into some badly worn tents provided by the Russians; where housing could be assigned, it was on the basis of six or seven people in each room.

Beyer needed help in handling the growing problem, which was threatening to sour morale among all concerned. Haywood traveled by train from Moscow to Kemerovo, departing in June and arriving on July 9, 1922. He brought more tents with him and provided them as emergency shelter during the summer and fall months. He also dispatched a cable to New York instructing the Organization Committee to send no more colonists until the spring of 1923.

During the spring of 1922, second thoughts were also being expressed in Moscow about the scope and cost of the Kuzbas project. Krzhizhanovsky, chairman of the State Planning Commission (Gosplan), presented a memorandum to the Deputy Director of the Council of Labor and Defense, V. A. Smolyaninov, recommending a reduction both in the number of workers to be recruited and in the amount of capital contribution from the Soviet Government. He recommended a total revision of the existing agreement. Rutgers returned to Moscow from the Netherlands to deal with this problem.

Precisely at this time, May, 1922, Lenin suffered his first serious attack of illness. His ability to support Kuzbas against doubters and opponents would henceforth be limited. His right hand and right leg were almost paralyzed and his speech partially impaired. At the insistence of his doctors he was moved to Gorky. In October, 1922, he was able to return to Moscow, but with severe restrictions on his work. He suffered a second attack on December 13, 1922, and another on December 16, 1922. The last time he worked in his office in the Kremlin was December 12, 1922. He lived at Gorky during most of 1923 and in October of that year suffered more attacks. He died of a cerebral hemorrhage on January 21, 1924.

The gradual removal of Lenin from an active participation in the direction of affairs was thus taking place in 1922 and 1923, the very years in which Kuzbas was established as a functioning colony. His impairment was always a negative factor in the background to the events we will see unfold. Rutgers had stressed from the beginning the vital importance of Lenin's active support to the project. That support could no longer be sought and utilized. In passing judgments on the successes and shortcomings of the Colony, certainly this unforeseen weakening in the guidance from Lenin must be accounted a severe handicap for the Colony and its leaders.

Probably on request from the Siberian Revolutionary Committee, Rutgers was advised of serious difficulties that were clouding the birth of the Kemerovo Colony. This set of problems now became more urgent than the discussions of contract revision going on in Moscow. Rutgers made preparations to travel east with his family in order to assume the general management of Kuzbas from its headquarters in Kemerovo. He arrived by train on or about August 1, 1922. We must now try to understand the complex situation that confronted him and Haywood in the summer and autumn of this first year of the Colony's existence.

We have a variety of sources to draw upon, who from their personal observations were able to report facts as they saw them. In the pursuit of accuracy and objectivity, it will be useful to refer to both friendly and unfriendly accounts. In the former category we have the reports of Haywood and Rutgers, who were sending their version of events and developments to the Organization Committee in New York. We also have letters from colonists who arrived in Kemerovo in 1922 as members of one of the first five groups. Among these Charlotte MacDonald and Anna Preikshas accented the positive aspects of the scene they described. So did Ruth Epperson Kennell, who arrived with the fourth group on August 25, 1922. She was a keen observer and a talented writer. She kept a very candid diary of day-to-day events, intending to draw on her experiences and impressions as material for stories and novels. She also wrote many magazine articles about Kuzbas for readers in the United States. At a later period in her life she wrote an autobiographical account of her years in Kemerovo, relying heavily on her diary and her recollections of events in which she had been a participant. This valuable document is probably the most interesting and illuminating of all sources with respect to the two years of her residence in Kemerovo. Though it has not been published, it is available in the Kennell Collection (see note 1).

Unfriendly accounts of the Kemerovo of 1922 are found in an article by Harry Harn (*American Federationist,* May 1923) and in interviews given to some New York newspapers by two other disappointed colonists, Samuel Goldstein and William Klohs. These three had been members of the first group to sail from New York. They arrived in Kemerovo in May, 1922, and departed in October of the same year. In December, 1922, on their return to New York, they related a bitter story which adds some details to the picture of life at the Colony in that first year.

Kemerovo in 1922

As Americans arrived by train at the station on the western bank of the north-flowing Tom River, they were always struck by the beauty of the shining river and by the high bluff that rose on the opposite shore, the mine side of the river. On the top of the bluff stood the finest house in Kemerovo, known as the Stone House. This had been built by Austrian prisoners of war to serve as the headquarters of the mine, with comfortable living quarters fitted out to accommodate two or three of the highest ranking officers of the company and their families.

There was no bridge across the river, so to reach the mine side passengers made the crossing in a ferry propelled by a paddle wheel that was turned by the endless walking of tired horses on a treadmill. Small boys with switches sat on the railing of the vessel to keep this horsepower at work. Overhead rattled the endless chain of coal buckets carried on cables stretched across the river.

Mounting the bluff on the right bank to the level of the Stone House, some 250 feet above the river, brought a fine view of cleared land stretching east to the edge of the *taiga,* the wild and marshy forest cover of Siberia. On the horizon could be seen low mountains, spurs that stretch north from the distant Altai Range. In the summer months wild flowers were abundant, giving some vivid colors to the drab village that had spread along both banks of the river. Streets were unpaved and frequently very muddy. Cows roamed freely through the village, grazing as they pleased. In many dooryards pigs, geese and chickens mixed with children and housewives. Most houses were decorated with branch weaving and with bouquets of flowers in windows. The meanest shanties were dug-out huts, makeshift dwellings half underground in the side of hills that bordered gullies emptying into the river. These were occupied by families of Tatars, who frequently added cheer to their quarters with lively accordion music.

Clustered around the mine-shaft structures were rows of houses built of logs, a kind of company-town for occupancy by mine employees. Back across the river to the west one could see the partially completed chemical plant with its towering chimneys. Around these two centers of work and construction were smaller auxiliary industries: a foundry, two machine-shops, a carpenters shop, a boiler shop, two brick kilns, a lime kiln, two sawmills and woodyards piled high with thousands of logs for timbering the mines.

Kemerovo was by no means devoid of amenities. There were coal-operated power generators on both sides of the river, so that most houses had a supply of electricity, more or less reliable. This was a point of contrast with other villages in the region where the only nighttime illumination was from candles and oil lamps. Water supply, however, was not quite so advanced. Since it was difficult to sink piping below the frost lines, water was delivered from house to house by "tank wagon", a barrel on sled runners.

Bathing took place in the river, and in 1922 freedom was still being celebrated by frequent bathing in the nude. Many Americans did not approve. For the more conventional, there were bath houses (with hot water) on both sides of the river. On one day a week these were reserved for women.

A small Orthodox church had been converted into a gymnasium. It was also still used from time to time as a center for celebrating the most important religious holidays. Though the priest had ceased to play a dominating role in village life, many houses still displayed icons or religious pictures on the walls of their living and sleeping rooms. These were still appreciated as interior decoration and still venerated by some for their religious significance. No

American account mentions the presence of priests in Kemerovo during the life of the Colony. If they came and went, they must have deliberately stayed away from the colonists, and the colonists from them.

On the mine side, a band shell in a plaza–like clearing became the scene of a concert by local musicians every week or two. A public meeting hall served as the theater for occasional amateur dramatic performances. On the chemical plant side (as the west bank was called) there was a larger and better-equipped theater, with a stage, settings and footlights. Performances there were the highlight of Kemerovo social and cultural life. Frequently, these were plays with a strong political content, aimed both at entertaining the audience and generating enthusiasm for the revolution. Russian classics were also undertaken. Patrons brought their own food and refreshments, prepared for long and convivial intermissions between acts. It was customary for these performances to last all night.

The town was served by a sizable hospital, with fifty beds, and by Dr. Nikitina Maria Vasilevna, a pre-revolutionary graduate of the University of Tomsk. She served as surgeon as well as general practitioner. In her role as physician on the Medical Commission (together with the local president of the Government Insurance Department and a representative of the Miners' Union), she had an administrative burden and a great deal of authority in making insurance awards, granting medical leave for illness and injury and in deciding on the allocation of housing. The arrival of American colonists added to her burden. The principal health problem of the community was dysentery. American victims were soon competing with Russians for beds at the hospital and for the attention of "Dr. Nikitina".

Poor sanitation was something of a shock to the arriving colonists. There was no sewer system. The population had to rely on community outhouses. Haywood described conditions as he observed them:

There are spots around the town that are little more than an immense dunghill. On the mine's side, between the bakery and the kitchens, a distance of about half a verst (about one-third of a mile), there is one place where, within the space of a hundred feet, there are four open toilet vaults. When a new hole has been dug, this filthy community backhouse has simply been moved the space of a few feet and the old hole left open, where the flies accumulate and later expurgate on food before it is consumed (*Kuzbas Bulletin,* Vol I, No. 7, of December 20, 1922, p. 7).

Haywood also reported that "every kind of vermin invade the houses in abundance." Flies and cockroaches were everywhere and especially in the kitchens. Among all observers there was agreement on the gravity of the sanitation problem and its negative effect on morale. An outbreak of typhus and the death of a four–year–old American girl from dysentery were further spurs to action. There was probably no greater service by the colonists to the inhabitants of Kemerovo in that summer of 1922 than their vigorous attack on the disease-spreading vermin and insects, and on the dunghills and open vaults. Several new holes were dug and new toilets built. The old ones were burned and lime thrown into the old vaults. These were then filled with dirt and more lime spread throughout the area. A war on rats and cockroaches began with formaldehyde and sulphur. Local jokes circulated to the effect that rats and cockroaches did not like the Americans and were taking refuge with the Russians. But Dr. Nikitina supported this campaign, and the Americans' ferocity, after being mocked, came to be admired and emulated. Haywood, with his characteristic enthusiasm, foresaw the day when "Kemerovo will be one of the healthiest spots in the world." He wanted it to become famous as a model of urban sanitation. It should be known, he said as the "spotless town". Here was small-town America producing some of its best effects where they were surely needed.

A cleaner supply of water than the river afforded was sought from springs and by digging new wells. A water supply tank was added to the design of the Community House and windmills ordered from the United States for pumping water.

The Kuzbas Coal Trust

The Stone House had all the basic modern conveniences, but it was filled with Russian occupants, and to remove them, or even some of them, was a delicate matter. Haywood chose to live in a tent and leave to Rutgers negotiations around that thorny question. Some of the occupants most likely to be inconvenienced were already the declared enemies of the new "autonomous colony."

They were representatives of the Kuzbas Coal Trust, which was managing the Kemerovo mine to their entire satisfaction when the Americans began to arrive with the intention of displacing the old management and introducing new techniques. The privilege of living and working in the Stone House was one of the first occasions of friction, probably inevitable, between the old *spetsy* and the newcomers.

The more fundamental question behind this friction was: were the Americans to be allowed to take over management of the mine, and if so, when? The Kuzbas Coal Trust, and particularly its Kemerovo personnel, were by no means reconciled to the decisions taken in Novo–Nikolaevsk and Moscow to approve this American intervention. With good reason, they saw it as a threat to their authority. To protect themselves they began a campaign to disparage the technical competence of the colonists to handle the task of running the mine. The New York Office had not been sufficiently careful in its selection of the first contingents, with the result that the few experienced miners and engineers were hardly conspicuous in the community of colonists. Unfortunately, some of the colonists made themselves look foolish by undertaking technical tasks for which they were not prepared. One of these was John Bebs, who incorrectly started a motor in a sawmill, ruined the machine and started a fire that damaged the building. This was made to order for the enemies of the Americans. A notice was issued, signed by Angevich, Director of the Kemerovo Region of the Kuzbas Coal Trust, which forbade all colonists to use any machinery until further notice. Undoubtedly a good deal of cultivated scorn and hostility toward the colonists complicated their problem in 1922. By the end of the summer, disillusionment was also being expressed in Novo–Nikolaevsk. When Rutgers passed through on his way to Kemerovo he was advised by Bazhanov, a Communist who had been named manager of the Kuzbas Trust, that "leaders consider it inexpedient to turn the Kemerovo facilities over to the colonists" (Trincher, 1967, 115).

One of the arguments used against the Americans was the image of anarchism conveyed by their style of work. Beyer's political formation was mainly influenced by his experience in the IWW. This was reinforced by the fact that Haywood's recruiting in Moscow among American workers and immigrants (mostly

Finnish) returning from the United States had focused on partisans of the IWW. Control at the work place by the workers themselves was their guiding principle. There was little experience to draw upon in putting the principle into practice, so discussion and argument over every detail were carried to extremes. Undoubtedly this slowed progress in housing construction and was at least partly to blame for the failure of the vanguard crew to have adequate housing ready as colonists arrived from the United States. Beyer was blamed for this, but the fact was that his authority was more nominal than real. As a matter of principle, nobody was in charge, and the results showed it. It was easy to find an occasion for ridicule in these practices, and even friends of the Colony, such as leaders and members of the Siberian Revolutionary Committee, could only deplore the frequent interruptions of work for general debate and the absence of a firm work plan.

Other frictions

We have already noted the ill will expressed by some of the spokesmen of the IWW in the United States toward the Communist leaders of the Soviet Republic. These polemics undoubtedly stimulated many of the IWW colonists to resist all efforts at organization wherever the Communists were playing a leading role. To some of these IWW missionaries, it was more important to test and implement their theories of industrial democracy than it was to please the Siberian Revolutionary Committee with a disciplined work effort. This problem plagued the Colony from its first days.

The arrival of new colonists from the United States did not bring a solution to the problem, because these contingents were also divided and sometimes sharply, between supporters of the IWWs and the Communists. The very large role that Calvert, Haywood, Beyer and Tom Barker had played in the creation of Kuzbas made it inevitable that recruiting would take place among IWW members and sympathizers. The fact that the Colony aimed to help the Soviet Republic made it attractive to Communists. Both groups volunteered and were shipped off together to Russia. It was unfortunate that the noisiest polemics between the IWW leaders and the Communist Party developed in the United States just as Kuzbas was being founded. This contradiction had to be worked out in the Colony, where the two groups were in daily contact with each other and often working side by side.

This cleavage in the Colony made everyone irritable and quick to find fault. The disunity among volunteers made it even harder to create an organization and an acceptable plan of work. Yet these were indispensable and urgent. Until they existed, morale would be low and the colony vulnerable to its enemies.

Where did Haywood stand in this controversy? Though he had been a founder of the IWW, he had more recently joined the Communist Party, and furthermore in Moscow he had come under the strong influence of Lenin and the Bolsheviks. He and Rutgers seem to have been in agreement that the anarchist tendencies in the Kuzbas IWW element would have to be tamed.

Progress

Haywood made some progress toward developing a plan of work during the month he was managing the Colony pending Rutgers's arrival in August, 1922. In addition to the sanitation measures already mentioned, he focused on two priority areas: construction and farming.

Work on the Community House was already in progress. Logs were available, and sawmills, manned by Russian workers, were operating on both sides of the river. With the arrival of colonists beginning in May and continuing through the summer there were more hands and more tools. Some colonists were added to the construction teams. Hours of work at the site increased from eight to nine hours, and a Sunday shift was created. These changes and assignments were preceded by ample discussion. The meetings were complicated not only by the political differences but by the fact that at least sixteen different nationalities were represented. It took time to establish working relationships based on mutual confidence and demonstrated competence. Mistakes were made in the assignment and acceptance of tasks, as in the case of John Bebs in the sawmill.

William Klohs, a farmer from Seattle, Washington, and another farmer from Milwaukee, Wisconsin, arrived in the first group. They brought with them a tractor, two plows and a packer. There were also shovels, hoes and spades. Though the Russian manager of the mines had a large supply of gasoline, he kept this hidden from the Americans and they were left without fuel for the tractor Nor were they allowed to use the horses from the mine stables. Prior to Haywood's arrival the colonists' efforts to start producing their own food had been limited to preparation of some garden plots. They had also explored the region where the Americans, under the agreement with Moscow, were to have the use of 25,000 acres for their agricultural needs. They had hired a peasant to plow ten acres.

Haywood arrived with several boxcars of equipment and supplies. Included were nine horses for Colony use, purchased with money advanced by the Soviet Government. He also purchased several wagons from local peasants.

When Klohs announced to Haywood that the farm team refused to use the horses and equipment because of their poor quality, it became clear that a serious problem of morale had to be confronted if the growing season was not to be lost. Klohs, a nonpolitical colonist, was embittered and expressed regrets that he had come. He and a few others of his team abandoned the farm and accepted assignments in construction.

Haywood then began to work closely with Jack Harper on the development of agriculture. Harper was an American IWW who had been among the first Haywood recruited in Moscow and sent to Kemerovo in 1921. Together they traveled thirty miles to the Kuzbas tract, surveyed its boundaries, selected sites for building houses and utility sheds and planned wells and an irrigation system. There was plenty of water on a year-round basis but summers could be dry. A camp for the reorganized farm group was established and construction begun. They found abundant grass for hay growing wild on the northwest sections of their tract. This would help in maintaining livestock.

A shipment of benzine from Petrograd arrived and provided fuel for the idle tractors. Then the other hidden caches already on hand were discovered and with much argument extracted from the mine manager. Fuel for the farm machinery was now available in good supply. Three other tractors arrived from the United States. Also, a good farm manager was found in Walter J. Lemon (sometimes identified as Walter J. Lehman). His previous experience had been in railroads, but with a willing spirit he undertook the job and proved his competence. (The Colony lost him in 1923 when he died from smallpox).

Several hundred acres were soon plowed and prepared for a crop of spring wheat. This operation greatly impressed peasants from the surrounding villages. Two Ford trucks were ordered from the United States. They were shipped in the fall and would be available for the following season. Plans were made to improve a road from Kemerovo to the farm. To begin with there was only a beaten path across a grassy plain and bridges across some of the streams.

Haywood located a tract of alluvial land a short distance upstream from Kemerovo village. This lay between the bluff and the river's edge. It was higher than the opposite bank and seemed to be safe from flooding. He saw it as an excellent site for vegetable gardens and orchards close to the Colony. It had a southern exposure and was protected by the bluff from northern winds. It would produce crops early. Irrigation in the dry months with water in ditches from the river would be easy. He found support among the colonists for this project and undertook to gain permission of Soviet authorities to utilize the land, which was not included in the original agreement.

To help the Colony feed itself, Haywood purchased six cows, four or five head of sheep and a few pigs. C. Van Erickson, a young farmer from Seattle had arrived with a dozen Rhode Island Red chicks and an incubator. More livestock would become available to the Colony with the management of the mine, but the date of that transfer was still uncertain.

With each contingent of colonists, the New York Office sent a shipment of foodstuffs equivalent to a two–years' supply. In addition each colonist (like all workers in the area) received a standard ration, called a *pyok,* of fresh meat from local supplies, potatoes and bread from a local bakery (which was soon supplemented by a Colony bakery). From the beginning the colonists were well fed. In this respect they were an island of privilege and regarded with some envy by many local residents. A custom developed of making gifts of food to visiting Russians and to fellow workers.

Charlotte MacDonald has provided us with a list of the dishes served in the Colony communal dining rooms, one on each side of the river: butter, cheese, tea, coffee, cocoa, canned roast beef, corned beef, sardines, salmon, mutton, honey, sugar, prunes, peaches, raisins, apples, split peas, beans, barley, rice, ham, bacon, spices and dried vegetables. In addition to milk fresh from the

Colony cows, it could be purchased from local suppliers who delivered it door-to-door all year.

The variety of nationalities in the Colony also added a variety to the dishes served. (Ninety percent of the colonists had been born in countries other than the United States.) Cooking responsibilities shifted from time to time from one nationality to another.

A symbol of solidarity

Perhaps this gustatory affluence made entry into the Colony an attractive prospect. Twelve marriages between single male colonists and Siberian girls had taken place by August 1, 1922 (*Kuzbas Bulletin*, Vol. I, No. 5, Sept. 20, 1922). Doubtless that fact, too, provoked some resentment among the male sector of the local population. But looked at in retrospect, Siberia was not losing daughters; it was gaining sons. Here was a higher stage of socialist solidarity across national lines. Most of these marriages proved stable, and where that was the case it was the beginning of a new family that stayed on permanently in the Soviet Republic. This was the history of Charles Schwartz, Jack Harper and Harry Sussman.

One of these marriages also brought Russians and Americans together in a shared grief. The Siberian bride of Bany Lucien, a colonist and miner, died not long after their wedding. Out of respect for her family and friends, Lucien had her corpse placed on display in the Russian style. Many Americans attended the funeral, finding it strange, but coming away with a deepened understanding of the people they had come to help.

Another tragic episode occurred while the third group of Americans was traveling by train from Moscow to Kemerovo. In those years a common sight was the *bezprizornie,* young vagabonds orphaned and cast adrift during the world war, the revolution and the civil war. One such youngster, either while begging or trying to mount the moving train, fell under its wheels and had a leg severed. The Americans and especially Charlotte MacDonald, a trained nurse, gave him emergency care and took him into their group. On arrival in Kemerovo, Bill Haywood took a special interest in the boy, who stayed on as a useful member of the Colony. He is the central figure in Ruth Epperson Kennell's novel for young readers, *Comrade One-Crutch.* (Harper & Row, New York, 1932). It is a story of life in Kemerovo, showing how the members of the Colony gradually came to feel themselves a part of the surrounding community. The book itself was an important event in the development of understanding between the peoples of the United States and the Soviet Republic. It was "fiction based on the facts," Ruth Kennell later wrote. It was also a charming expression of the human solidarity which Kuzbas came to symbolize.

5

REVISING
THE AGREEMENT

By the time Sebald Rutgers arrived in Kemerovo in August, 1922, it was clear that the dimensions of the Kuzbas project had been revised in fact from those envisaged at the time the agreement was signed in Moscow in October, 1921. From data compiled by the American Organization Committee we know that three hundred and two male workers were dispatched in 1922. There were also approximately 100 working wives and 80 children, or a total of nearly 500 colonists. Some of these (approximately 80) were sent to the Bogoslovsk region, the remainder to Kemerovo. To these numbers must be added the vanguard contingents sent from Moscow in 1921 and early 1922. By the autumn of 1922 the colony at Kemerovo would have numbered approximately 430 persons. There had been some departures, however, before the arrival of the last group in September. The population of the Colony stabilized at approximately 400, later arrivals just about balancing departures over the next few years.

We have seen that some of the reasons for this *de facto* revision in the project were to be found in the difficulties and handicaps of the American Organization Committee. Other reasons lay in the economic and political conditions in the Soviet Republic, especially a severe capital shortage, the illness of Lenin and opposition to change from the old managers and technicians.

Rutgers had reason to be discouraged under these disappointments, but that was not in his character. He came prepared to do battle, both with the internal problems in the Colony and with its enemies in the old administration. The dimensions of the project had shrunk but not its importance in the mind of Rutgers. With his arrival, a new authority was in place, and this began to work its effects both on the colonists and on the representatives of the Kuzbas Coal Trust.

Rutgers lodged his wife and children at Tomsk and prepared himself for work without distraction. He was accompanied to Kemerovo by Bronka Kornblitt, the Polish Communist who served as his secretary, interpreter and aide. She was in frail health, but she had a will of iron, and she too believed in the importance of Kuzbas. She was literally to give her life to the cause. All colonists who have described her agree on her intense dedication to her work and her total loyalty to Rutgers. She was undoubtedly an enormous help to him.

Since it is inevitable that many readers will wonder about the sexual aspect in their relationship, this account must prove a disappointment in that respect. They lived in the same house in Kemerovo, the Stone House, but in separate rooms and under the observation of other tenants. A simplicity and asceticism in their personal lives complemented their total dedication to the demands of their work. But they were also warm and human, capable of anger and other expressions of emotions. Perhaps there is a love story there, but if so, it will have to be invented from the imagination. No observer has left us any record of fact or opinion. All we have is a letter from Rutgers to his wife with the following enigmatic passage: "I cannot deny that Bronka is not indifferent to me and I cannot be at ease knowing that you are suffering. Therefore it is better for the three of us to be together as little as possible. The things they say about us should mean nothing" (Trincher, 1967, 146).

Rutgers was aware (through his friend Heiman) of the aura of romanticism that characterized the recruiting effort in the United States. He also knew from the Siberian Revolutionary Committee of the impression created by the IWW lumberjacks and carpenters sent with Beyer from Moscow. Rutgers had written an article for publication in the *Kuzbas Bulletin,* (May 22, 1922) which clearly expressed his views of the errors and the weaknesses in the initial stages of the project. The article also announced what would be the spirit of his direction as manager at Kemerovo. He couched his ideas in a series of statements as to what Kuzbas was *not* to be:

1) It is not an autonomous empire. It is an integral part of the Soviet Republic under the supervision of the Council of Labor and Defense. Those who do not believe in the Soviet Republic should not volunteer.

2) It is not a place for theorists and dreamers about a future society. It is to be a place of *work*.

3) It is no place for those who insist on receiving the full product of their labor. This will be treated as a social product and will belong to the people of the Soviet Republic.

4) It is not a cooperative. It is not a path to personal wealth.

The aim of this article was to discourage applications from sympathizers with an IWW ideology. Its tone was strikingly different from that of the Prospectus, drafted by Calvert and Barker. Rutgers's article appeared too late to have any effect on recruitment of the first two groups of colonists (which had already sailed); and probably it had little or no effect in countering the influence of Calvert and Barker on the recruiting effort during 1922 in the ranks of the IWW. This opposition from Rutgers to the further recruiting of syndicalists was a major factor in his changing attitude toward Calvert and Barker.

The two big and urgent problems Rutgers confronted on arrival in Kemerovo were interrelated: how to overcome the anarchy which was distracting the Colony and how to introduce the colonists into the going enterprises of the Kuzbas Coal Trust. These enterprises (for example, the mine) had not been turned over to the AICK (Autonomous Industrial Colony, Kuzbas) and were still being managed as if there had been no agreement with the Americans.

Rutgers received strong support from the local Party organization and from trade union leaders. But he knew there were some Communists in the Siberian Revolutionary Committee (e.g. Bazhanov) who doubted whether the agreement was going to produce the hoped-for results. When Bronka Kornblitt privately expressed her indignation to Rutgers at the opposition from the old *spetsy* and even from some Communists, Rutgers said "we will have to show our technical competence and ability to organize" (Trincher, 1967, 115).

Perhaps the arrival of Rutgers and the steps he took to introduce order and discipline in the Colony convinced the Coal Trust official, Angevich, to modify his policies. He consented to consult with Rutgers about utilization of the Americans, and Rutgers consulted with Haywood. Gradually these three formed a functioning triumvirate. The order denying the colonists access to machinery was rescinded. American miners were admitted to the mine shaft to work alongside Siberian miners. And one of the sawmills was in effect turned over to the Colony, since it was to be entirely manned and supervised by colonists and devoted to their projects.

Autonomy settled

The principal construction task in progress was on the Community House. Rutgers was appalled at the lack of planning and clear responsibilities. Hours were spent each day in discussions and democratic votes on technical questions. He blamed these practices for the slow rate of progress.

Haywood was a key man in introducing reforms; since he had recruited many of these workers, he understood their IWW ideology and he had been working with them on the project since his arrival in Kemerovo. Haywood did not want to lose any workers; yet disillusionment, discontent and defection were in the air. Some IWW workers felt oppressed by the atmosphere in Kemerovo and in the whole Soviet Republic, which was more and more infused with a spirit of Bolshevik discipline. Resistance to it, whether in the name of rank-and-file democracy or anarchism had become suspect. It had become an established truth that anarchy was an enemy to be overcome. Haywood undertook the task of reconciling these sons of the IWW (many of whom were still opposed to all governmental authority) to the reality of the Soviet Republic. His policy was to work with the men as they were, to participate in their discussions, to accept the resulting delays and argue against any suggestions of defecting from the enterprise.

The colonists were divided among themselves, so that Haywood in seeking to placate some was offending others. According to Goldstein and Klohs there were strong resolutions adopted at Colony meetings during the month of July 1922, "condemning the management of Haywood."

Rutgers adopted a different approach. He had felt the negative atmosphere that was developing toward AICK in Moscow and in Novo–Nikolaevsk. To him the Colony faced a crisis which had to be confronted and clearly resolved without ambiguity. If this meant losing some colonists, in his view that was a lesser evil.

The fundamental first step in redressing the situation was to establish the subordination of the Colony to general Soviet policy. The word "autonomous" had been construed by some to support the notion that the colonists were free to adopt policies according to the wishes of the majority among them and also to elect their own managers. There was no support for such an interpretation in the words of the agreement negotiated between the Council of Labor and Defense and the "initiatory group". However, in a document entitled "Statute of Organization and Provisions on the Basis of the Agreement with the Council of Labor and Defense of the RSFSR (Russian Soviet Federative Socialist Republic), it was stated that within six months "after the first groups arrive from America", the original Managing Board would be replaced by a Board of members selected by the workers in the colony, "subject to the approval of the Soviet authorities" (See Appendix B). This document, according to Calvert, was drafted by Lenin. It also contained the Lenin pledge. The third clause in that pledge contained the statement:

> The members of the Unit pledge themselves in case of misunderstanding or conflict, that they will accept as final the decision of the highest Soviet authority in Russia.

It will be recalled that the word "autonomous" as a descriptive name for the Colony originated with Lenin. The content of that word as he used it is illuminated by the Statute of Organization. (There seems to be no reason to question Calvert's assertion that Lenin drafted the Statute.) Lenin apparently wanted to convey in printed form his wishes as to the way the Colony was to be managed. The Statute was presented to Haywood, Beyer, Barker, Calvert and Rutgers for their signatures, which they executed on October 22, 1921, one day after the signing of the Agreement itself. The Statute was not signed by any representative of the Soviet Republic. Calvert brought a copy of the Statute with him when he returned to the United States in November, 1921. Every colonist recruited by the American Organization Committee was asked to indicate acceptance of the Statute by signing a copy.

On the basis of this Statute, the colonists certainly had reason to expect that sooner or later they would be electing the Managing Board of the Colony, always "subject to the approval of the Soviet authorities." This is apparently what Lenin envisaged. He must have expected a spontaneous and voluntary respect on the part of the colonists for Soviet policies (deriving from a careful selection by the Organization Committee). On this assumption they could be trusted to elect their own managers.

The bitter denunciations of Soviet policy by the IWW leadership in the United States, and the large number of IWW members and sympathizers in the emerging colony brought Rutgers to the conclusion that the Statute was a dead letter. Rutgers had gone through a rude awakening since October, 1921. The recruiting had not gone as he expected. Opposition to an autonomous industrial colony of foreign workers had proved to be potent and subtle in Kemerovo and in Moscow. At least in part due to that opposition, progress in preparatory work had been slower than anticipated. Coordination among New York, Kemerovo and Moscow had been difficult and deficient. Dissension and bad morale among the colonists had fed doubts as to the wisdom of the big capital investment involved. The spirit of the New Economic Policy was being implemented at all levels. It was a time of severe realism and criticism of all romanticism in previous Soviet policies. In this Moscow atmosphere an enthusiasm for AIC Kuzbas was an anomaly, an anachronism from an earlier period.

Rutgers's policies represented the adjustment of Kuzbas to that new reality. Rutgers did not wait for a formal modification of documents. He knew that would come later, providing the Colony could prove its ability in practice to survive in the new circumstances.

The arrival of Rutgers therefore marked a decisive turning point in the history of the Colony. Within a few weeks he changed the expectations of the colonists. So far as we know, Haywood made no objections in Kemerovo to the changes Rutgers began to implement, although he could not have had the enthusiasm for the new prospects which he had originally felt and expressed in Moscow in 1921. Rutgers spoke with an authority that only he possessed, an authority based on the confidence reposed in him personally by the Council of Labor and Defense. Rutgers regarded that confidence as defining his primary responsibility. With such a manager "autonomy" ceased to be a problem.

It is rather interesting to ponder the fact that a Dutch Communist thus emerged early as the manager of AICK at Kemerovo. He was to hold that position until 1925 when he was replaced by a Soviet Communist. This certainly has to be considered in any characterization of the nationality of the enterprise. Haywood would return to Moscow a few weeks after Rutgers's arrival and would be replaced on the Board of Managers in a reorganization soon to come. The old Indian IWW warrior, Beyers, died of a heart attack during a colony meeting on October 4, 1922. (His grave is in Kemerovo.) Thereafter Rutgers recruited many of his leading assistants from Holland and from Germany. In popular conception Kuzbas was an "American colony". It takes nothing from its symbolism as an inspiring example of international solidarity to point out that Americans (of various national origins) were henceforth participating, alongside other foreigners, in a Soviet enterprise.

According to Klohs, Rutgers called a meeting of the colonists to announce that he was taking charge and that with two Soviet assistants from Novo–Nikolaevsk he would appoint directors of the different activities. It is probable that Rutgers had discussed the situation at the Colony with the Siberian Revolutionary Committee and was now endeavoring to regain its confidence by giving it a more direct participation in the supervision of activities. Rutgers also announced to the colonists that they would not be permitted to elect managers or officers.

From the Trincher biography of Rutgers, we have a picture of the new manager trying to change the anarchistic work style of the construction crew by appointing a Dutch construction engineer, A. Baars, as foreman, and giving him authority to organize and discipline the crew. Rutgers himself was probably the biographers' source for the following account. Baars, with Rutgers's support, tried to put a stop to the needless meetings for discussion of technical questions. Baars, who had worked in the Dutch colony of Java, was blunt: "To the devil. You are supposed to do as I say. Enough chattering. Here I decide."

To this workers retorted: "He's a damned planter. Treats us like Indian coolies. Grab him boys! Throw him in the river!"

Bronka Kornblitt saved the situation: "Comrades! Comrades! We must work together, workers and engineers. Comrades, you should subordinate yourselves!"

Rutgers supported Baars: "Discipline—that's the main thing." He let it be known that anarchism would no longer be tolerated. To Bronka he referred to his task as "putting bridles on a crew of wild horses."

In another episode recounted in the same biography, Rutgers and Haywood had assigned a room in the Community House to one of the women of the Colony to serve as a sewing room as well as her living quarters. She discovered that three miners had taken over the room, and when the woman showed them the signed order they scoffed at it. Rutgers directed Bronka to convoke a general meeting of the Colony. Haywood chaired the meeting and called on Rutgers.

Rutgers: The question here is discipline.
From the hall: We are sick of discipline!
Rutgers: Three colonists seized a room by force in the Community House, against an order signed by Rutgers and Haywood. They will have to give up that room now.
One of the miners: We are miners. We need rest. Here comes a sewing lady. Gets a good room.
From the hall: Right! Right!

Haywood tried to restore order, and someone called for a vote, "Who is for the miners?" A forest of hands went up.

Rutgers: You interrupted me. You decided the question on your own. You decided not to subordinate yourselves to the rules of management. So you will have to vote again.

Rutgers looked at Haywood. There was a total silence.

Rutgers: Haywood and I have decided to resign from management of the Colony unless you agree to honor and obey our regulations.
(Silence in the hall)
Rutgers: I ask that a vote be taken.
One of the miners: We will give over the room. We did not think about it that way. We are for discipline.
Voices: Yes, discipline!

All hands went up in support of the management order. The meeting ended.

Later Bronka asked Rutgers, "And if they had voted against you?" Rutgers replied: "I was sure. You see, we have good material here".

Some discontented colonists depart

Rutgers had decided not to let tact weaken the impact of the changes he was demanding. Some were defiant and submitted their resignations. On August 26, 1922, a notice was posted on the bulletin board to the effect that twenty-four resignations had been accepted. The list included names from the advance crew and from each of the first four groups that had arrived from the United States. Some, for example, Otto W. Rae and his wife, had been in Kemerovo for only two weeks. Free transportation would be provided to the border of the Soviet Republic plus one month's supply of food. Rutgers and Haywood signed papers asking the assistance of all comrades in arranging the departures.

On September 4th, 1922, the discontented ones boarded a train in Kemerovo to begin their return to the United States. Their transportation to Petrograd was paid out of Colony funds. There they remained in a hotel for six weeks free of charge (apparently at the expense of the Soviet Government). They were fretful and impatient, but some Soviet officials were against allowing them to depart in violation of the terms of their contract. It took an intervention by Rutgers during a visit to Moscow in October to resolve the issue in the Soviet Foreign Ministry. They left the Soviet Republic on November 4th, 1922. Their return to New York was of course a blow to the morale of the American Committee. It was evidence that insufficient judgment had been employed in choosing the colonists.

In a letter to the American Committee, Rutgers explained his view of the situation. He blamed the Committee for failing "to reduce and improve" the "transports from New York. We may even consider to return the fifth group on the same vessel that brings them." He cited the case of a tailor, Israel Per, one of the returnees. "What the hell do we want here with a man qualified only for a modern tailor shop?" This man had been misled and should receive a refund of the $1,000 he had paid to the Committee. The others should receive no refunds. (In fact Calvert did pay them small sums, e.g. $35 and $50, to help them find other means of support).

Ruth Epperson Kennell arrived with her husband in Kemerovo in August, 1922, in the fourth group of colonists. We are fortunate to have her eyewitness impressions of this period of crucial change.

She set them down in an article written in October and published in *The Nation* of January 3, 1923. She and her husband Frank had been close to IWW circles in the United States and undoubtedly sympathized with IWW visions of a truly autonomous industrial colony functioning in fact under the sovereign control of its own workers. But Mrs. Kennell viewed the situation with an open mind and no party commitment. In time Rutgers won her over (though not her husband). In the article she wrote after two months in Kemerovo she dwelt on two themes: (1) The positive prospects and plans of the Colony to expand production and (2) the different character of the Colony from what she had expected. She referred to Rutgers as a "practical, bourgeois engineer". In line with the New Economic Policy of the Soviet Government, she wrote, Kuzbas Colony "will be a capitalistic enterprise under state control." She was not critical of this turn in events, but she cautioned her readers:

> The type of rebel that answered the call for pioneers to help the Workers Republic will not be content with such a consummation to fit into this program.

That prediction is an indication of a mood among the colonists at that time. Actually, things turned out better than she foresaw. Many such "rebels" did adapt to fit into the new program, as we shall see. But another one of her conclusions proved to be entirely accurate:

> . . . the importation of workers from America, except certain specialists, will cease. The romantic period of Kuzbas colonization is a closed book.

Getting organized

Rutgers also had to deal with the problem of convincing Soviet authorities that the Colony could make a solid contribution to production of material goods for the Soviet market. To the Council of Labor and Defense this was the reason for the Colony's existence. It would have to see tangible results if the Colony's life was to be extended.

Rutgers was fortunate in the arrival with the fourth group of Alfred Pearson, Jr., a mining engineer with extensive experience. He had been a Captain of Engineers in the U.S. Army. He held master's degrees in engineering, and he had been Chief Engineer at Pennsylvania May Coal Company. Politically, he had long been a believer in socialism, and he welcomed this opportunity to put his expertise to work in the Soviet Republic. Pearson and his wife, who took on work in the Colony kitchen on the mine side, soon proved themselves valuable assets to the Colony and continued so during their three-year stay.

The Kuznetsk coal basin provided a challenge to Pearson. It is wedge-shaped, about 80 miles wide and 250 miles long. Running south from Tomsk it reaches almost to the Telbess ore field, the most important iron deposits in Siberia. The coal field had been worked commercially since about 1900. Sales in the past had been made principally to the Trans–Siberian Railroad, to the Ural metal plants and to a small local domestic and miscellaneous industrial market. At times as many as a dozen mines had been in operation. In the chaos of revolution and civil war, the market had shrunk and in 1922 work was concentrated at four mines, among them Kemerovo.

The Kuznetsk mines were in an advanced stage of disintegration. Supporting uprights of poplar wood were rotten and dangerously weak. Ventilation was poor and frequently nonexistent, so that gas masks had to be donned on entry. There was so much water seepage that rubber boots had to be worn. The few pumps no longer worked. Miners had no cap lamps, but had to carry oil lamps by hand.

Pearson wrote down his observation of the labor force working at the Kemerovo mine:

Russian labor is composed of both whites and Mongolians, the latter mostly Tartar . . . they have been kept by the former government in absolute ignorance and illiteracy . . . the wage scales have been consistently set on a piecework basis so low as to force the men to put in a full day for a bare existence. It is said that before the war the foremen also used the lash to drive the men. The natural reaction of the worker now is to still further limit the production. . . The piecework system is applied to every class of work. This requires not only extra accounting and the consequent extra time keepers, but also, when applied to the repair shops and miscellaneous outside activities, a staff of estimators to set the rates for the smallest jobs. And this is not to mention the endless bickering which inevitably arises over wages. The custom of furnishing tools and working clothes calls for an extensive warehouse and staff. (*Coal Age*, Vol 28, No. 22, November 26, 1925, p. 725).

There was also still in effect an "artel" system in which a large group of men contracted to do a job together, their pay being based on the group's production. Pearson learned that Russian engineers had spent their lives trying to break up the artel system because it made discipline impossible. The practice of loafing was general, each worker suspecting the others of doing the same.

This was the combination of material and organizational handicaps which, in Pearson's view, explained the low rate of productivity per man-day in the Kuznetsk mines: one tenth of a ton. Everyone agreed that ought to be raised. The "initiatory group" had undertaken to the Council of Labor and Defense to raise production by raising productivity per worker. Pearson gained Rutgers's confidence as one who could play a key role in enabling the Colony to meet that commitment. He used Pearson's presence and the arrival of other experienced miners (among them Alex Nemmi, Albert Meissner, William Lugge and John Preikshas, the latter a Lithuanian immigrant recruited in the United States) as arguments to the Siberian Revolutionary Committee that the Kemerovo mine should be turned over to management by the Colony. The Kuzbas Coal Trust engineers were opposed to this, and it would not take place until February, 1923. In the meantime the American miners, now numbering about 35, were allowed to work together in a reopened shaft, the Vladimir.

Frank Kennell, a former Unitarian minister who had prepared himself for Kuzbas by studying the accounting system used by an American mining company, began to work with the Russian accountants at the formidable task of mastering their system and improving it. His wife, Ruth, became a secretary in the Colony administration and Colony librarian.

The Americans had brought several boxcars of equipment, food and materials from the United States. More had been provided by Soviet authorities (for example "shubas" and "peemies", the long sheepskin coats and felt boots that would be indispensable in the Siberian winter). The task of issuing and maintaining a control on these stores was assigned to Simon Hahn, an American Communist. He also proved to be a great asset in the Rutgers administration. Rutgers came to refer to him as "the irreplaceable Hahn."

Natalie Ortt, also known as "Kevah", became head of the Commissary Department. She had left her husband and home in

Wichita, Kansas. She was a bright spot in the lives of the colonists. "Mellow as Indian summer" and "playful as a kitten", she took charge of feeding the Colony and became known as "the Pyok Queen".

Samuel Shipman, a Cornell University graduate in Management Engineering, was named director of plans. He had been unable to find a job in the United States, so he signed up with Kuzbas to seek experience and adventure. Ruth Kennell described him as a "level-headed idealist, neither communist nor wobbly".

The Colony had a well-trained specialist in William H. Mahler, a doctor in chemical engineering from the University of Vienna and Zurich Polytechnic, recruited in Newark, New Jersey. He had been well chosen to lead the work at the chemical and coke-manufacturing plant. His credentials were also an argument for approving an American takeover of management. The plant's construction had been commenced by a French and Belgian concern, Kopikus, before the war. Now it would have to be completed, equipped and set into operation in the production of such coke by-products as benzol, naphtha, creosote and dyestuffs, useful in the dye and medical industries. How long this would take and the quality of the results would also be a test of the Americans. This chemical plant was to be the first in Siberia. Mahler was eager to take over authority from the Russian director of the plant, Stankevich, and move forward rapidly; but money would be needed, and its availability depended on decisions in the Soviet Government. Nothing was certain in that time of change.

The American committee replaced

In response to a telegram summoning him to a meeting of the Council of Labor and Defense, Rutgers, accompanied by Bronka, traveled to Moscow in early October, 1922.

Lenin did not attend the CLD meeting, and the President of the Planning Commission, Krzhizhanovsky, presided. The question was whether to authorize continuation of the Kuzbas Industrial Colony or terminate it.

Engineer Fedorovich, the former director-manager of Kopikus, presented figures to show that "under present conditions it is not possible to turn the AICK into a profitable enterprise" (Trincher, 1967, 121). He argued that only foreign capital could save the situation in the Kuznetsk Basin and that the Kemerovo mines should be turned over to a foreign capitalist concession. Another engineer, Rabinovich, manager of the coal industry as a whole, also presented a report calling for an end to the Colony.

Rutgers, of course, argued against these opponents and pointed out that the independence of the Colony from foreign capital was of positive political significance (which had always been one of Rutgers's principal reasons for establishing the Colony). He also stressed the competence of the recently arrived technical personnel, the new organization measures, progress on the farm with the new tractors, the establishment of work discipline and departure of the worst troublemakers.

After listening to these debates, Krzhizhanovsky stated that the Planning Commission favored continuing development of AIC Kuzbas and would give the Colony all possible support. It would be necessary, however, to make some changes in the agreement. This view was adopted as the CLD position.

Rutgers was greatly relieved. He was prepared to modify the agreement. A major part of the problem, in Rutgers's view, was now to be solved. He had lost all confidence in Calvert and Tom Barker, who were running the American Organization Committee. The official policies of the U.S. Communist Party and the IWW not to give formal support to the work of the Committee defeated the purpose of the nine-member structure of the Committee. Rutgers had to accept that reality. (He was being kept informed by Julius Heiman.) He asked that two of the liberal (independent) members of the committee, Thomas Reese and Mont Schuyler, rather than Calvert and Barker, be sent to Moscow to discuss changes in the agreement with the CLD. They arrived about October 15, 1922.

Discussions began among Rutgers, Haywood, Reese, Schuyler and representatives of the CLD. An unpublished manuscript by Mellie Calvert is our source for a report on those discussions. She got her information, including written minutes, from Schuyler or Reese on their return to New York.

Rutgers, with support from the CLD representative, Bill Shatov, wanted to reduce the Managing Board from fifteen to three, to be located in Moscow, Kemerovo and Nadezhdinsk. In effect this would end the American Organization Committee. Haywood was opposed to this change and so was Schuyler. Haywood argued, according to the minutes of the meeting held on October 28, 1922:

> The members of the Managing Board who now happen to be in Russia are, in my opinion, in no way authorized by the Statute of the Colony to take the drastic action which the motion entails.

Reese held the view (shared by attorney Roger Baldwin, another member of the Organization Committee) that AICK had always been a Soviet enterprise and that Soviet authorities were free to change it as they wished. Reese added a third vote to those of Rutgers and Shatov and joined in the preparation of the proposed changes for submission to the CLD. (Mellie Calvert was very bitter toward Reese for what she considered a betrayal of the American Organization Committee.)

The Council of Labor and Defense proceeded to ratify the Rutgers–Shatov–Reese initiative by appointing a new Board of Management, "in the persons of Comrades Rutgers, Reese and a representative of the Council of Labor and Defense." (CLD decision number 366, date unknown, quoted in the Mellie Calvert manuscript.)

P. Pascal Cosgrove, another member of the American Organization Committee had arrived in Moscow too late to vote against the new proposal. He did join with Haywood and Schuyler in addressing a communication to the Council of Labor and Defense, dated November 14, 1922. This stated their views as follows:

> 1) The original agreement and statutes of the colony should be preserved unaltered.
>
> 2) This calls for the election of a Managing Board in Russia by the colonists in the near future. . . .
>
> 3) Also the continuance of the present Organization Committee in America until their work is completed. . .

This communication produced no practical effect. A letter from Rutgers to Calvert dated November 18, 1922 stated:

> S.T.O. (The Council of Labor and Defense) has appointed a new managing board of three, Reese, Rutgers, and Shatov, since 14 members all over the world is no working proposition. The New York Organizing Committee will now be an apparatus of the Russian Managing Board and fully under its control. Nobody can be sent to Russia unless asked for and this includes all the members of the Organization

Committee. A copy of the new agreement I will send as soon as it is ready, and Reese will come with instructions and full authority to arrange matters in New York. The period of propaganda is over and we have to come to business, restrict all expenses to a minimum until the arrival of Reese, who will come immediately after visiting Nadezhdinski Zavod (Works) and Kemerovo.

At another meeting on November 21st, Rutgers stated that he had no confidence in Calvert and Barker and that the American Organization Committee was to be dissolved. Schuyler was told that his services were no longer needed. Schuyler canceled plans to accompany Reese on an inspection trip to the Colony and instead returned to New York. The new Managing Board, composed of Rutgers, Shatov and Reese, began acting under its new mandate. In effect, Haywood, too, was dismissed. Since the CLD had ratified these changes, a new agreement was drafted and signed on December 25, 1922.

Recruiting of technically trained personnel was to continue in the United States. Therefore the new Managing Board had to have its representative there. Reese was the one American who understood the new regime and sympathized with it. He was sent back to the United States with authority to take over direction of the New York office. This fed Mellie Calvert's suspicions that Reese had joined with Rutgers and Shatov in Moscow in order to make himself number one in New York. Under the reorganization both Mellie and Herbert Calvert would be losing their positions.

Meanwhile in Kemerovo

Meanwhile, back in Kemerovo, the colonists were enjoying crisp Siberian autumn weather and expanding their social life and contacts with the local population. They held their first party in a schoolhouse with dancing and games. The Russians and Tatars watched, curious, and then entered. All enjoyed refreshments of black bread and jam.

Ruth Kennell organized a players' group and staged a first offering, "Supressed Desires" highly appreciated by the audience of colonists and locals at the Narodny Dom (People's House).

The wedding of Abraham Siegel, an American electrician, to a Siberian girl, Dusa Abdavena, took place on the left bank. The bride was arrayed in American clothing lent for the occasion.

Frank Kennell read the wedding service, making no reference to a deity "in order not to offend the Communists" (some were militantly anti-religious). There were wedding-drop cakes and cocoa, and luscious tomatoes donated by a Siberian guest. Late at night the mine-side residents rowed back across the river in bright moonlight, singing. There were good things happening in the midst of troubles.

The first snow fell on October 6th. Colonists discovered that their sheet iron stoves drew badly. Broken window panes could not be replaced. Electric power failed almost every night and lights went out. The colonists sang songs to keep up their spirits, while a cold wind from the fast-freezing river whistled through cracks and around doors and windows.

As the days grew shorter and the weather colder, a hot steam bath in one of the public baths was a much-enjoyed luxury. There was plenty of coal for heating the water. A Canadian master mechanic, John Kask, took his first steam bath without finishing off with cold water before emerging into the frigid air. He caught pneumonia and died in November, 1922. His funeral and that of Jack Beyer saddened the Colony and brought it closer together.

During Rutgers's absence in Moscow, the Russian managers of the mine stepped up their campaign against the Americans. They rescinded the order that turned a sawmill over to the colony. Also, Angevich gave notice to three American families to vacate a certain cottage, which was to be used as a labor union headquarters. Reaction to this among the colonists exacerbated the serious divisions among them. Communists took the position that Angevich's action was justified. The IWW's were indignant and called a protest meeting. They made fiery speeches saying that American workers were being exploited in a foreign country by local bureaucrats backed by American Communists. An IWW Local was created and Ruth Kennell, to her surprise, was elected secretary.

Mining Engineer Pearson and his wife became involved in a row with Simon Hahn and his wife. To make room for a new Russian mining engineer, Pearson ordered the Hahns to give up their quarters in the Stone House. They refused, quoting a Soviet law that tenants could not be evicted in winter. The two wives, in particular, were at swords' point. Hahn resigned. Frank Kennell sent a letter to Rutgers in Moscow:

The situation is critical. Applications for release from the colony are coming in daily, led by the IWW's. . . All of us recognize the necessity of employing bourgeois specialists, but to give a reactionary such as Pearson power to humiliate and harass sincere and competent revolutionary workers can only end in complete disruption.

A telegram from Rutgers ordered Hahn to return to work, and he complied. A tense peace was restored, and a valuable supply officer was saved.

Disgruntled IWW's handed in their resignations and refused to work. A few days later a notice, signed by the Russian Chief Engineer, was delivered to their barracks by a militiaman informing them that their *pyok* would be taken from them if they did not return to work.

The Colony meeting on this crisis was the stormiest in its history. Irreconcilable differences broke out in impassioned speeches and bitter personal attacks. The motion before the meeting was to deprive those who refused to work of their food and other supplies. The Communists supported this motion, and it carried. The Wobblies argued: We have paid for our *pyoks;* we put in thousands of dollars we won't get back; Kuzbas is worse than a prison camp; we are held against our will and without food. One Wobbly (Neef) broke into song: "For might was right when Christ was hanged."

A Finnish Communist, Jokilheto, yelled: "Shut up, you dirty counterrevolutionary dog!" Neef whirled and struck him in the face. Jokilheto drew a dagger. Someone else drew a gun. Several others held and disarmed them.

Frank Kennell supported the Wobblies:

This project was misrepresented in America as an opportunity for the IWW to make a constructive contribution to the Russian Revolution. . . The IWW's feel that they must either choose to accept wage slavery in a state capitalist enterprise, controlled from above, or to go home. They are choosing to go home.

Ruth Kennell refused to support her husband on this issue, and they quarreled bitterly. But Ruth was also exasperated by the "narrow-minded bigotry" and the display of a "self-righteous sense of power" by some of the Communist colonists.

But that night in their barracks, the strikers voted to return to work. They said that was because a majority of their fellow workers had so decreed, and not because the management had ordered it.

There were other altercations with less political content. Ruth Doyle of Baton Rouge, Louisiana, slugged the colony schoolteacher, Amy Schechter, because the two Doyle children had been sent home from school for misbehavior. Mrs. Doyle and her husband, Thomas, worked in the warehouse and were suspected of stealing goods. They added their names to the list of discontented colonists who wished to return to the United States.

One of Rutgers's first acts on his return to Kemerovo from Moscow was to approve the release of those who wanted to leave, granting them free transportation to the border and food for one month. The Doyles chose to be transferred to Nadezhdinsk.

Rutgers brought the good news that the Kemerovo mine and chemical factory were to be turned over to Colony management on February 1st, 1923. The Soviet Government had approved a credit of two million gold rubles (equivalent to approximately one million dollars) to enable the Colony to go forward with its plans. The Colony had weathered the trials of its first year, a year full of difficulties and some disappointments. Now with a new lease on life, Rutgers brought a determination to complete the Colony's adjustment to its new status and demonstrate its ability to produce efficiently for the Soviet economy.

Rutgers had been engaged for months in clearing away all ambiguity regarding the subordination of the Colony to Soviet law and authority. On his return to Kemerovo following the period of reorganization and renegotiation in Moscow, he announced that the workforce would be divided into the seventeen categories then utilized in other Soviet industries for pay purposes. Actually, the change did not have any significant effect on the colonists' income, since sixty percent of their pay would continue to go into a common fund for support of the commissary, from which all enjoyed identical sustenance out of supplies sent from the United States or purchased in Siberia. Nevertheless, the malcontents seized upon the announcement as evidence that their expectations were being betrayed and that Rutgers was converting Kuzbas into a capitalist enterprise. This loose use of the epithet, "capitalist", could not stand up under scrutiny and it was not long before the new system became an accepted feature of Colony organization. (There were naturally some complaints over individual assignments to specific categories.) A few departing IWW's added this offense to their table of grievances. Others accepted the change with the good humor of Harry Sussman, the Colony's wittiest comedian. He propounded the slogan: "Workers of the world, unite, and be divided into seventeen different categories."

The change was a good one in that it furthered the process of incorporating American workers into the ranks of Soviet labor and made them participants in a common structure of organization regardless of national origin. This process was hastened by the admission of colonists into Soviet labor unions according to their work specialties. The Communists from the U.S. took part in meetings and activities of the Siberian section of the Communist Party (Bolshevik). This included attendance by colonists at Party conferences held in Petrograd, Tomsk and Shcheglovsk. The great majority of the colonists studied Russian, developed lasting friendships among the people of Kemerovo and took a great interest in the history and culture of their new world, so different from what they left behind in the cities and towns of the United States. Already the Kuzbas enterprise had shown that, while the Americans might have some difficulties in getting along with each other, there were no barriers dividing them from the peoples of Siberia!

This developing solidarity among American and Russian workers impressed Cosgrove and Reese when they visited Kemerovo in January, 1923. They brought with them to the United States a sample of its expression. It was a resolution passed on January 21, 1923, by the "American Miners of the Kuzbas Colony in Kemerovo, affiliated with the All-Russian Mine Workers Union." It read in part:

> We . . . hereby send to the American Workers, especially to the Miners of America, a hearty greeting and thanks for the donations made to the American Colony such as tools and presents, etc., which we believe were not only a helping hand to the American Colonists, but in reality a help to build the industries in Russia. . . . We, the American Miners of the Kuzbas Colony at Kemerovo, Siberia, are working in the best

spirit. . . . We came here for the purpose of helping to build up industry and not for personal profit. . . . Again, greetings to the revolutionary workers of America, with hopes for the early establishment of the World Workers Republic.

Ephriam Kentta
William Lugge
Leo J. Wydra
Abraham Seigel, Chairman

(*Kuzbas Bulletin,* April 1, 1923).

This was still the spirit of Kuzbas after its year of trials and setbacks! The defection and departure of a minority of misfits (not more than 50 out of a total of 458 colonists) improved morale and strengthened everyone's determination to put petty differences aside and make a success of their historic undertaking.

6

NADEZHDINSK WORKS

In the vision of Rutgers and Calvert, formed during their inspection journey to Kemerovo and the Ural Mountains in the summer of 1921, the Bogoslovsk region in the northern Urals, which included rich iron ore deposits and the Nadezhdinsk Works for making iron and steel, was to serve as an adjunct to the coal, coke, chemical and agricultural production of the Kuznetsk Basin where Kemerovo was located. The two regions were connected by the Ob River and by railroad. In this plan, which Rutgers had outlined in his report of September 12, 1921, to the Council of Labor and Defense, coal from the Kuznetsk mines, once production exceeded the needs of the Trans–Siberian Railroad, would be converted into coke at the Kemerovo chemical plant. This coke would be shipped to the Nadezhdinsk Works in the Urals for use in the extraction of iron from its ore and for the manufacture of steel and machinery to be used in the modernization of agriculture and the development of Siberian industry. Lenin had accepted the thesis that the two regions complemented each other, each promising to supply the needs and utilize the product of the other. This Faustian vision conformed to the grand dimensions of the geography of its setting, the desperate needs of a people and the boundless confidence of a victorious revolutionary leadership. Conceived in the euphoria of dawn, the vision was incorporated into the Agreement of October 21, 1921, between the "initiatory group of American workmen" and the Council of Labor and Defense.

Rutgers and Calvert had found excellent plants and equipment at the Nadezhdinsk Works, including seven blast furnaces and nine Marten ovens (for the production of pig iron), an automatic rolling mill with its own power plant (for producing railroad steel) and a mill for the manufacture of tin plate. There were also many massive steel reinforced auxiliary buildings, some with forges, presses and lathes imported from Europe and the United States. Most of these facilities, some of the best in Russia, were standing idle and deteriorating due to a shortage of skilled labor and paralysis in the managers, who were confused and doubtful as to their prospects in the emerging economic and social order. Rutgers and Calvert could envision these plants quickly brought to life and productive efficiency by skilled American workers and engineers recruited to the Kuzbas enterprise. In drafting the Prospectus, Calvert and Barker used the figure of three thousand men as a minimum needed to commence the operation at Nadezhdinsk Works which, they wrote, "is to be the machine shop of Kuzbas."

In the review and revision of the Kuzbas enterprise that began in Moscow in the early months of 1922, the inclusion of Nadezhdinsk was one of the features immediately subjected to scrutiny and challenge. This review was taking place in the State Planning Commission (Gosplan). Undoubtedly the preemption of the productive potential of the Nadezhdinsk Works resulting from its dedication to the Kuzbas project provided grounds for protest in the Planning Commission, which had responsibility for planning economic development throughout the new Republic. The Commission could not be pleased at the loss of control over such a major asset in the existing national inventory of plants and machinery. The Commission's desire for a revision of the Kuzbas Agreement had some support in the Council of Labor and Defense, evidenced by the fact that Bill Haywood was told in the spring of 1922 by Bill Shatov, who represented the CLD in the original Managing Board of the Kuzbas enterprise, that Nadezhdinsk should be eliminated from the project. Haywood resisted this suggestion, and a heated argument ensued. This episode, reported in a letter from Simon Berg, a Communist assigned to work at Nadezhdinsk, sheds light on the later course of developments involving the Nadezhdinsk connection. (The Berg letter, dated November 22, 1922, is reproduced in Mellie Calvert's unpublished manuscript.) A tug of war was going on inside the

Soviet Government for control over Nadezhdinsk, the most modern and highly developed complex assigned to Kuzbas under the 1921 Agreement.

We have already noted the opposition to an American takeover in Kemerovo mounted by the Russian managers and specialists of the old regime, who resisted a change that would surely leave them demoted in authority if not displaced. The same kind of interested opposition was of course at work against implementation of the Kuzbas project in Nadezhdinsk. Berg's letter also gives an insight into the ability of the existing management, threatened by the presence and pretensions of arriving Americans, to generate an atmosphere of skepticism and hostility which added enormously to the difficulty of winning the confidence of Russian workers. Berg's judgment had a basis in the facts he observed: there was deliberate sabotage of American efforts to restore and improve operation of the plants from Russian managers and specialists who then used the disappointing short-range results as arguments against the feasibility of American plans for the future development and utilization of the Works.

The engineer whom Calvert and Barker recruited in the United States to represent the Kuzbas project in Nadezhdinsk, William Van Hoffen, sailed from New York with the first contingent of colonists and arrived in Moscow in May, 1922. Since he was a nonpolitical engineer and knew no Russian, he was assigned a Communist aide, Berg, who knew the United States well and who had accumulated valuable experience since the Revolution as administrator of Moscow bakeries. Berg had been in Nadezhdinsk since February, 1922, as a member of an advance party sent to make preparations for the arrival of recruits from the United States. Fired with enthusiasm for Kuzbas, he met Van Hoffen in Moscow. They then departed for Nadezhdinsk, accompanied by four other colonists and Van Hoffen's wife–secretary. In the United States, recruiting for Nadezhdinsk was proceeding, hampered by all the difficulties encountered by Calvert and Barker previously described. Of the 458 recruits sent to the Soviet Republic by the American Organization Committee in 1922, approximately 80 were assigned to Nadezhdinsk.

A letter from another member of the advance party, "Fellow worker Marsukevich, late of the San Francisco IWW local", was published in the first issue of the *Kuzbas Bulletin*. It contained some detailed descriptions of facilities and conditions at Nadezhdinsk. He reported that "one of the high furnaces out of seven is working, but with minor repairs three of the others could be put to work. This would increase production six times. One Martens furnace out of seven is working, but four more can work with slight improvement." Marsukevich also reported that many houses in the area had running water and electricity; there would be housing for at least one hundred fifty families on their arrival from America (a much more favorable situation than that existing in Kemerovo).

The following paragraphs from Marsukevich's letter express the optimistic assessment of a member of the vanguard reporting on prospects as he saw them:

> You are probably aware of the cold officiality displayed by the old management towards us. However, do not get the impression that all the people are such. On the contrary they believe that we are their whole salvation from the misery, want and misfortune that entangle them at the present time. They anticipate better conditions for themselves; they deserve it, too. When we arrived they surrounded us in the mill and asked us when we will take the plant over. "As soon as our fellows arrive from America," we said. "When will that be?" they asked again. When we replied that perhaps after a few months, they all sighed and said, "By that time we may all be dead here." As soon as our fellows set to work gathering together the house repairing material, the rumor spread that the Americans were going to repair all houses. . . .
>
> To keep good hope in us, and in the workers here, and to show them that we are really going to do real good work, do your utmost to get plenty of the right boys from America. Let Calvert and Barker keep us informed as to whether there are sufficient class–conscious workers in America who are interested as they ought to be in the problems confronting the Russian working class, and who are prepared to work alongside of them. We are sure that with 250 qualified men from abroad, including specialists and engineers, that we will be able to take over this plant without any trouble or any hitch.

Perhaps Marsukevich was right in his opinion that "250 qualified men from abroad" could do the job. But events were taking place which foreclosed the possibility of testing his prediction. Berg came to the conclusion a few months later that the battle to keep Nadezhdinsk in Kuzbas had already been lost in Moscow before Van Hoffen arrived on the scene. It is true that Van Hoffen stepped into a task of rehabilitation in which a potent combination of forces was working against his success. The old *spetsy* were determined to prevent him from accomplishing anything which might justify and strengthen the friends of Kuzbas in Moscow. What infuriated Berg was not opposition from the *spetsy* in Nadezhdinsk (this he regarded as natural and inevitable, one of the obstacles to be overcome) but the readiness of members of the Planning Commission to take these biased reports of the *spetsy* as grounds for reconsidering the attachment of Nadezhdinsk to Kuzbas. Van Hoffen, despite his excellent technical qualifications and experience in steel manufacture, was totally inept in his role as champion of the Kuzbas plan in the committees and corridors of Moscow. He was vulnerable to rumors (spread by Shatov, according to Berg) that he was a counterrevolutionist who wanted to use Kuzbas as a disguise for bringing in American capitalist influence. Berg, who lived and worked closely with Van Hoffen in their shared trials, scoffed at such a charge. But he does depict Van Hoffen as a baffled and miserable failure in his Moscow appearances as advocate before skeptics. By the end of the summer of 1922 (four months after his arrival) Van Hoffen was in a state of nervous exhaustion. He was unable to prepare a crucial report on progress and plans at Nadezhdinsk for presentation to the Planning Commission as it began considering proposed revisions of the Kuzbas Agreement in September, 1922. According to Berg, Van Hoffen got drunk in Moscow and "acted like a crazy man." Postponement of his appearance before the Planning Commission was requested and granted. Negative judgments on Van Hoffen became arguments for severing Nadezhdinsk from Kuzbas. If there had been another Rutgers at Nadezhdinsk, perhaps the outcome would have been different. Van Hoffen's performance also undermined confidence in the competence of the American Organization Committee that had recruited and chosen him for such a key position.

In early October, 1922, with the arrival in Moscow of Reese and Engineer Schuyler from New York and Rutgers from Kemerovo, an attempt was made to assist Van Hoffen in preparing his report and presentation. This was still not adequate to win a majority in the presidium of the Planning Commission. A telegram from Subotin, Chief Engineer of the Bogoslovsk Trust, charged that repairs to a gas engine made by the Americans in Nadezhdinsk were proving ineffectual. He alleged that the Americans were "creating panic in the Russian workingclass masses." Again according to Berg, "Van Hoffen, in reply, could not come back at them because he was shaking like a baby, nervous and near a breakdown." Bogdanov, Chairman of the Supreme Economic Council, and Lomov, Chairman of the Ural section in the Planning Commission, advocated removal of Nadezhdinsk from the Kuzbas Agreement. This position was adopted by the Planning Commission presidium.

Rutgers fought like a tiger in this verbal melee and wrote an article for *Pravda* in his campaign to win support for a reversal by the Central Committee of the Communist Party of the decision in the Planning Commission. His stand in these discussions was that efforts to implement the Kuzbas plan should be concentrated in the years 1923 and 1924 on developing Nadezhdinsk along the lines envisaged in 1921, even if this meant cutting back on funds for Kemerovo (*Kuzbas Bulletin* of January 20, 1923, p. 2).

Rutgers was successful only in delaying the outcome. The Council of Labor and Defense decided not to rule on the question of Nadezhdinsk's status for another year. This was said to be at the request of the Kuzbas Managing Board. This "request" was undoubtedly motivated by a certainty that any present decision would have removed Nadezhdinsk from the Kuzbas project. The immediate effect was to leave Nadezhdinsk under the control of its Russian managers headed by Baron Traube and to deflate the hopes of the Americans who remained there. Van Hoffen was dismissed though not disgraced. He had indeed impressed many observers with his competence as a metallurgical engineer. The CLD found other work for him first at the Petrovsky Works at Baikalsk and later as Chief of the Concession Board of the Far Eastern Republic, where he stayed until returning to the U.S.A. in 1924. Berg was also reassigned to other Party work and removed from participation in the Kuzbas project. He had been too extravagant in his defense of Van Hoffen and too one-sided in his condemnation of what he called "the Kaisers and Kings who put the Kuzbas on the bum." He described himself as "nervous wreckage." He was truly a casualty, a fallen soldier, in the ill-fated battle to keep Nadezhdinsk in Kuzbas. Feeling "cast aside as a dangerous and damaging element", he wrote to Calvert and Barker: "I will go to the place where my Party will direct me, but in mind I will be with you."

Rutgers was more circumspect and put as brave and calm a face as possible on a serious setback. In his written reports on the Moscow decision he touched on the Nadezhdinsk aspects only lightly, saying that no adequate inventory, proposals and budget had been prepared for presentation to the Moscow authorities and that the year's delay would be used to repair that deficiency in the Kuzbas performance at Nadezhdinsk. This was a leader's whistling in the dark in order to keep up morale in a period of sweeping readjustment then being implemented in Kemerovo and New York as well as Nadezhdinsk.

The handling of the vacancy created by Van Hoffen's dismissal showed that Rutgers had drawn the conclusion by the end of 1922 that Nadezhdinsk was lost. The new Managing Board created by the modifications of the agreement in November and December, 1922, was to number three persons: Rutgers for Kemerovo, Reese for Nadezhdinsk and a representative of the CLD stationed in Moscow (for the time being, Shatov). On its face this seemed to promise a serious effort to hold on to Nadezhdinsk, with Reese striving to become the Rutgers of the Urals. In fact, when Rutgers advised the New York office in November, 1922, that the CLD had abolished the old Managing Board and created a new one consisting of Reese, Rutgers and Shatov, he stated in the same letter that Reese would quickly be returning to the U.S.A. "with instructions and full authority to arrange matters in New York".

This is exactly what took place. Reese made an inspection trip to Nadezhdinsk and to Kemerovo with Pascal Cosgrove and then returned to take charge of the New York office. There was apparently no intention of sending him to Nadezhdinsk as a replacement of Van Hoffen. He was never recalled to assume a post there. It is also noteworthy that Mont Schuyler who had accompanied Reese to Moscow for the reorganization meetings, was not sent to Nadezhdinsk to fill the vacancy left by Van Hoffen. The inference is strong that Rutgers, having read all the signals in Moscow, was shrewdly readjusting his own sights and accepting the loss of Nadezhdinsk, at least for a period of some years.

Such a readjustment was by no means fatal to his plans for Kemerovo. In the Kuznetsk basin at a distance of one hundred miles from Kemerovo stood the Guriev steel works, hampered by lack of raw material and skilled workers. And not far to the south, much closer to Kemerovo than were the Ural Mountains, lay the still undeveloped iron ore deposits of the Telbess region.

Here was a convenient combination from which a "machine shop for Kemerovo" could be created out of materials closer at hand and not so important to Moscow's plans for industrial development in other regions. The Faust in Rutgers did not despair. In the excitement of his on-the-spot survey in 1921, Rutgers had been carried away by the impressive installations at Nadezhdinsk. In incorporating the Bogoslovsk region into their proposal to the CLD, he and Calvert had been misled by their own zeal into biting off more than they could chew. Those were the hard lessons taught by the experience of 1922. An article appearing in the *Kuzbas Bulletin* of April 1, 1923, summed up these lessons as follows:

> It is now more fully realized that a greater length of time must elapse before the projected program can be fully attained. The possibilities are unlimited and have a tendency to run away with the imagination, such vistas are presented. But the sober realist also sees the innumerable difficulties that are to be surmounted, the obstacles that must be overcome, and the organization work ahead before Kuzbas can proceed by its own momentum.

Henceforth Rutgers concentrated all his energies on the Kuznetsk basin and let Nadezhdinsk go its own way. The need for a team of engineers and skilled workers to conduct a survey at Nadezhdinsk and prepare the promised report to Soviet authorities was published in the April, 1923, issue of the *Kuzbas Bulletin,* but no actual search for applicants was undertaken. By the middle of 1923, with no formal announcement, it was an accepted fact that Nadezhdinsk had been dropped from the Kuzbas vision. There was too much to do in the Kuznetsk to leave time for regrets.

The Americans who had been sent to Nadezhdinsk in 1922 gradually adjusted to their growing isolation from Kemerovo. Some stayed on under the Russian managers; others transferred to

Soviet projects in other regions; some returned to the United States. In June, 1923, a resolution of the Council of Labor and Defense directed that those Kuzbas colonists still remaining in the Urals should be reassigned to Kemerovo. The *Kuzbas Bulletin* of July 29, 1923, mentions that Greenberg and Arberg had arrived at Kemerovo from Nadezhdinsk.[8]

7

DISSONANT VOICES

Throughout this period of shakedown in the Kuzbas enterprise, the major American news media were titillating the public with indignant reports and commentary (frequently blended in the same tendentious columns) regarding the deplorable conditions of life encountered by the Americans who had volunteered to work in Siberia and the Urals. Correspondents were always ready to report and editors to embellish the complaints of returning colonists. This was valuable propaganda material in the campaign directed by the government from Washington to discredit the Soviet government in the eyes of the American people. This form of "Cold War" had already begun with the aim of keeping Americans from responding, with instinctive feelings of sympathy and humanity, to the great revolution in Russia. Washington was deeply committed to an overthrow of Bolshevik power; the President and his cabinet chafed under the restraints placed on them by public opinion.

The Kuzbas enterprise was an offense because it circumvented the guardians of the social order in the United States and urged Americans to go directly to the Soviet Republic, whether Washington liked it or not, and establish their own friendly relations with the peoples of Russia and Siberia in a stirring demonstration of international solidarity. Such an enterprise would help the Bolsheviks consolidate their authority; it would strengthen their lines of communication with the American people; it would improve the climate of world opinion toward the Bolshevik revolution. Each of these promising aspects of the Kuzbas enterprise was seen as an affront by the governing powers in Washington and New York.

The boldness of this generous initiative was captivating, as were its defiance of hardships, its independence of action, its sense of history-in-the-making and its appeal to an honored pioneer tradition. Kuzbas was seen as an expression of revolutionary will, originating in the American people, an enthusiastic declaration of faith in a new economic and social order that predicted the demise of capitalism.

Such an appraisal sounded an alarm in the capitalist press and touched off its campaign to make the enterprise appear a laughable failure or a criminal conspiracy to defraud innocent victims. The complaints of some of the returning colonists, anxious to justify their own defections, provided newspapers with just the material they wanted for guiding public opinion in the desired direction. Any malcontent who would denounce the enterprise could be assured of an audience and sympathetic support from editors and authorities.

Not many of the returnees allowed themselves to be used in this way, but a few did (some six or eight out of the fifty who returned in 1922 and 1923). The New York *World* published a series of articles in March, 1923, based on material provided by William Klohs and Samuel Goldstein. The phrasing of the articles betrays an intent to generate revulsion in the reader for the enterprise being described. If Klohs and Goldstein had anything good to say about their experience, it was not allowed to appear in the very one-sided descriptions of suffering and regret published over their names.

These distorted accounts produced sadness and resentment among those who knew the true facts, which overall provided grounds for optimism despite the hardships and disappointments. Alex Nemmi, a Communist and miner, wrote to Mulari from the Colony: "When you see parties who left dissatisfied, do not pay much attention to them. . . They did not come to Kuzbas to rebuild Russia but only to help themselves".

The collaboration of public authorities in this campaign to ruin the Kuzbas cause became evident when the District Attorney in New York City, Emory C. Weller, brought charges of grand larceny against all the members of the American Organization Committee. In this maneuver he had the full cooperation of Thomas Doyle and his wife, Ruth, of Baton Rouge, Louisiana. The Doyles had been at odds with most of the other members of the Colony from the day of their arrival in Siberia. When they requested transfer from Kemerovo to Nadezhdinsk they were under a cloud of suspicion of theft from the Colony warehouse. They stayed only a few weeks in Nadezhdinsk and then requested return to the United States, where they arrived on April 4, 1923, eager to have their vengeance while enjoying the comforts of New York. Public opinion had been prepared by Klohs, Goldstein and the New York *World* to give them a sympathetic welcome. The Doyles communicated their grievances to the Department of State in Washington, and it may have been from that quarter that the suggestion came to make contact with the District Attorney.

Despite the fact that the District Attorney had absolutely no evidence (not even in the form of allegations by the Doyles) that any of the money collected by the American Organization Committee had been pocketed by Committee members, Mr. Weller was able to utilize the cooperating press to generate some scandalous headlines. He obtained warrants for the arrest of Pascal Cosgrove and Thomas Reese, and once they were brought in he gave to reporters the allegations that the Doyles had paid in their $1,100 as a result of false representations made to them about conditions in Siberia and the Urals. The New York *World* captioned its article based on this material: "Two Held as Family Tells of Starving in Russian Colony." *The New York Times* headline read: "Starved, Robbed, Back From Russia." (April 7, 1923) The following is an excerpt from the *Times* story:

> They were sent here and there, their money was taken from them and starvation threatened them until finally they were able to get out of Moscow.
>
> The worst of all experiences, according to Doyle, was the constant insult offered to his wife by Soviet officials and others who sought continually to convert the colonists to the principle of free love.

The truth or falsity of these sensational tidbits did not affect their impact on an uninformed public. The Doyles seemed to have been the only colonists to whom Soviet officials advocated "free love" and the only colonists who were not eating well out of Kevah

Ortt's abundant supplies. A reader who knew the singularity of these charges might well have suspected they were deliberate inventions either of the Doyles or the District Attorney. But they served their purpose, which was to undermine confidence in Kuzbas and its promoters. The District Attorney proceeded to obtain indictments charging all nine members of the Organization Committee with grand larceny. As witnesses before the secret session of the grand jury, he presented the Doyles and three other disgruntled colonists, Anton Novak, Edmund J. McGuire and Otto Rae.

One of the indicted defendants was Roger Baldwin, founder and member of the Board of the American Civil Liberties Union. Fortunately for all the defendants, Baldwin was well known as a man of high integrity, and his reputation with the public raised doubts as to the grounds for a charge of grand larceny. Arthur Garfield Hays, a respected New York attorney, suspected that the District Attorney was using the judicial process for making political propaganda on the government's behalf without any basis for a criminal prosecution. He acted as representative of all defendants before the Court after satisfying himself that the books of the Kuzbas Committee accounted for the expenditure on transportation and supplies of every dollar received from colonists. Judge Alfred J. Talley evidently shared doubts about the legitimacy of the proceedings and granted Hays's motion for an examination of the grand jury minutes. These showed testimony by the complainants to the effect that they had paid in a certain amount of money on representation of conditions which they claimed did not exist. Hays then moved for a dismissal of the indictments.

Five months passed before Judge Talley granted Hays's motion for dismissal as to all defendants except Cosgrove. Hays then moved for an immediate trial of the Cosgrove case, intimating to the Court that he believed the District Attorney was trying to delay a trial date with the intention of never trying the case at all. After a few more months of delay the Judge also dismissed the charges against Cosgrove.

The American Civil Liberties Union conducted its own investigation of the charges and issued the following statement:

> The prosecution is obviously inspired by hostility to all enterprises for the aid of Russia. It is exceedingly unlikely that any such charges would have been brought on a similar showing by colonists returning from anywhere else in the world. . . .
> The only question at issue is whether there was misrepresentation in

the original prospectus. A committee of this organization [the ACLU] has examined the prospectus, together with the pledge signed by every colonist who went to Russia. The committee finds that these documents specifically warn prospective colonists of the hardships to be endured and the difficulties to be faced, that they define and limit the responsibility of the management in cases of discontent, and that their detailed frankness is *prima facie* evidence of good faith. . .

It is easy to see why the District Attorney was not anxious to go to trial with such a case. Every colonist, including these complainants, had signed the Lenin Pledge, which specifically referred to the hardships inevitable in the rehabilitation of industry in a very backward and devastated country. The Committee of the ACLU expressed the further opinion:

The books show that the money paid in was spent principally for the colonists' own transportation and equipment. It is of course an extraordinary proceeding to charge grand larceny under such conditions. Usually such claimants would be referred by the District Attorney to the civil courts to recover whatever damages they could prove.

The Doyles did not have enough confidence in their case to take it to a civil court (which would have required them to hire their own lawyer). They were content to let the District Attorney use them through the newspapers. They enjoyed notoriety for a while and accepted invitations (for example, from Samuel Gompers of the American Federation of Labor) to present their case without any risk of cross-examination.

This attack on the Organization Committee came at a time when it was being dissolved as a result of the revisions of the Agreement with the Council of Labor and Defense that were effected in Moscow in the last months of 1922. Herbert Calvert had acquiesced ir. the reorganization there agreed to by Rutgers and Reese and removed himself from the Kuzbas office in April, 1923. His departure together with his wife, Mellie, implemented the decision taken in Moscow that Reese was to assume direction of the New York office. Tom Barker was no longer a member of the Managing Board, but he did stay on as a salaried employee in charge of publicity including preparation of the *Kuzbas Bulletin*. Matti Mulari and Pascal Cosgrove, former members of the Organization Committee, also stayed on as salaried staff members in the New York Office.

Calvert and Barker had been the authors of the Kuzbas Prospectus which was now under attack in the District Attorney's
propaganda campaign. To vindicate its accuracy, Barker asked
Alfred Pearson, the mining engineer who had been in Kemerovo
since August, 1922, to send to New York his written opinion of the
Prospectus in the light of his experience in the Kuznetsk basin.
Pearson had no party commitment and no political axe to grind, so
his response is worth quoting at some length:

> Re your recent request that I look over the Kuzbas Prospectus and give
> a professional opinion as to its accuracy of statement:
>
> If I were to write a prospectus myself using the data at my disposal
> after nearly a year's intimate knowledge of Kemerovo, I fear that it
> would sound much more extravagant than the one put out by the
> American Organization Committee.
>
> The resources at the disposal of the American Colony are so stu-
> pendous as to excite the imagination. The Kuznetsk Basin according to
> the best available information contains valuable mineral deposits of a
> far wider range than mentioned in the Prospectus. The coal is conser-
> vatively reckoned to constitute one fourth of the known world coal re-
> serve. All the above added to a truly marvelous soil and a not impossible
> climate, await proper direction, energy and machinery from the colonists.
>
> I have carefully read the prospectus through and in so far as Kemerovo
> is concerned—I am entirely unacquainted with any other places—I am
> unable to find any statements which I could characterize as either
> overstatement of fact or deliberate mis-statements.
>
> In detail I believe it is as accurate as it would be possible for a
> non–technical man to get from a tour of inspection, such as was the
> basis for the document in question.
>
> The only possible criticism I can voice is that a person acquainted
> with a modern American town, reading the Prospectus, would of course
> be unable to visualize the drab appearance of a Siberian town of log
> houses, and might be disappointed by the actuality, although I have
> seen many mining camps in America, compared with which Kemerovo
> is a dream city.
>
> I am sorry I can't make this sound less like a white-wash from an
> interested party, but after jotting down in detail every error I could
> pick out, the list sounded so puerile that I am compelled to give the
> above statement.

News of the District Attorney's actions and the Doyles's allegations evoked indignation among the colonists, many of whom took

steps to place on record their repudiation of the charges against the Committee. Following is the text of a resolution passed by the American Section of the All-Russian Mine Workers Union of Kemerovo on June 21, 1923:

Whereas, one Thomas B. Doyle and others, formerly members of the Kuzbas Organization, after returning to the United States of America gave out certain public statements and filed certain information with the District Attorney of the State of New York;

And whereas these statements made public and the information given the District Attorney of the City of New York as reported in the American press and reported to us in private letters were all false and misleading:

And whereas it is untrue that Russian conditions were misrepresented to members joining the Kuzbas Colony, that the members have been deceived or swindled in any way or that there was any shortage of food or that the colonists were compelled to endure other undue hardships and discomforts as stated by the aforementioned Doyle and others:

Therefore, be it resolved, that we American members of the 'Kuzbas Colony' here assembled, reaffirm our faith in the mission to which we have pledged ourselves, and in our persecuted representatives in New York City, and hereby brand as false the statements of Doyle and his kind and protest the arrest of our representatives and the publication of such misleading articles in the American press.

One more detail in the events precipitated by the Doyles manifested the division in the Soviet Government over the value of the Kuzbas enterprise at the end of its first year. Charles Recht, a New York attorney, was acting as representative in New York of the Society for Technical Aid to Russia. He was also acting as legal adviser to the Soviet government on problems arising in the United States. He had been empowered to issue visas to persons wishing to travel to the Soviet Republic. The District Attorney sent an assistant and detectives to Recht's office and escorted him to the jail where Reese and Cosgrove were being held following their arrest. Reporters attributed to Recht statements (which he never took the trouble to rectify) in which he denied any connection with the Organization Committee (that was unfortunately the truth) and added that the Kuzbas Colony was practically discredited by the Soviet government. Recht's failure to give the Committee his support in this crisis helped the District Attorney in his press campaign to undermine confidence of the public in the Committee. This episode suggests that Rutgers's efforts in Moscow to win solid support for a revised Kuzbas project had not been entirely successful. It also suggests that some of the doubts, some of the skepticism, which Rutgers had had to overcome in winning approval by the Council of Labor and Defense of a new budget for Kemerovo were still working against the Kuzbas officers in their labors of recruitment in the U.S.A.

By the time Calvert departed, the principal agency for recruiting, besides the *Bulletin,* was the series of "Kuzbas groups" he had established in approximately twenty-five cities from the East to the West Coast, including groups in Ontario and British Columbia. The majority of these were in Pennsylvania, Ohio, Illinois and California. In each of these groups one or two individuals acted as local representatives of the enterprise with a responsibility to keep the groups informed of developments and needs. They collected money, tools, books, food and clothing for shipment to the Colony, and they helped candidates prepare their applications and arrange travel to a point of assembly, usually New York. These groups held meetings to hear letters written by colonists telling about their reception and travels, their reactions to what they had observed and their lives in Kemerovo or the Urals. Occasionally there were talks by visitors from the New York office, especially Calvert, who made the promotion of these outlying groups his principal activity.

A clear change in the tone of the recruiting campaign took place at beginning of 1923, connected undoubtedly with the reassessment that had taken place in Moscow and the emergence of Rutgers as the dominant conductor of all Kuzbas activities including those in the U.S.A. This change was conveyed to all groups by a page in the *Kuzbas Bulletin* of February 20, 1923, entitled "New Forces Needed." This announced more rigorous standards of selection than hitherto required, with an emphasis on technical expertise and experience. Job descriptions were set out in some detail, for example:

ONE FARM MANAGER

Preferably a man with college experience. Must be used to economical large-scale farming. Good executive. Must have had extensive farming experience in Canada or Northern States.

ONE TRUCK GARDENER

Again a man who is used to a Northern climate with plenty of experience. Applicants should write in detail their experience and enclose copies of testimonials, etc. They should also state when they are ready to leave and upon what terms they are prepared to go. Single men are preferred.

CIVIL ENGINEER

Architectural Engineer or architect, over 30, capable of directing general construction work, including buildings.

The list named some two dozen different specialties for which there were openings for a total of ninety-two people. The announcement included a cold corrective to the ardor of enthusiasm: "Persons are requested not to make application unless they are certain that they are thoroughly competent to fill the position for which they are applying." Each applicant was asked to state upon what terms he or she would be prepared to leave for Siberia for a three years' engagement. Technicians were now being sought to the exclusion of ordinary workers; therefore the prospect of favorable financial remuneration and perquisites was used to evoke interest, a change from the previous year when there was an appeal to class solidarity with Soviet workers and to a vision of "the first industrial colony in the world, . . . where workers will find that self-government, that sense of social creativeness, that solidarity and equality they have never found anywhere in the history of the world until this present hour." The striking difference between the recruiting strategy in 1922 and that in 1923 reflected the difference between Calvert and Rutgers. As Ruth Kennell had advised from Kemerovo, the romantic period of Kuzbas was closed.

Reese returned to the United States in the spring of 1923 with Rutgers's authority to recruit experts by offering to pay them well. Rutgers was not calling for a large number of recruits. He wanted only skilled workers and a few qualified people to fill key technical posts. He had grown accustomed to directing an enterprise in which the great majority of workers (about nine out of ten) were from the local population, and he had decided they did not need the inspiration and example of class-conscious fellow workers from more advanced countries so much as they needed direction and supervision from trained and educated experts and from skilled and experienced workers as foremen. With the substitution of Reese for Calvert this was the reorientation that took place in the recruiting effort. This new emphasis continued to dominate recruiting for the remainder of Kuzbas's existence even after Reese departed in 1924 to be replaced by Barker. The IWW philosophy of Calvert had been quietly but permanently discarded.

After the dissolution of the American Organization Committee a new Advisory Committee was created. The following accepted membership:

Dr. Charles P. Steinmetz of the General Electric Company
Walter N. Polakov, economist and engineer.
James H. Maurer, president Pennsylvania Federation of Labor
Leroy Peterson, cashier of the Amalgamated Bank of New York
Morris L. Ernst, New York attorney
Roger N. Baldwin of the ACLU

In his letter accepting membership, Dr. Steinmetz wrote:

> I am very much interested in Kuzbas and hope much from it.
>
> Everybody taking interest in the enterprise knows or should know that it is the creation of a better world in which he is taking part, but that he goes out into a field where he must expect hardships and disappointments, where he must organize and create. There are always a few people who imagine that in such an enterprise they will drop into a safe berth and have a good and easy time, and then get disappointed and come back and throw mud, after they have met the reality.

The first contingent of colonists to depart in 1923 sailed from New York on May 2nd. It numbered approximately thirty persons, including five children. Two more small parties left New York in June and July and two others left from San Francisco in July and August, 1923, for travel to Kemerovo via Japan and Vladivostok. These arrivals, according to a census taken in Kemerovo in November, 1923, restored the Colony population to 318 adults and 82 children, a total of 400 people.

8

In Kemerovo there was rejoicing over the news that the Council of Labor and Defense had approved a transfer of control of all local production facilities from the Russian managers to Rutgers and the Kuzbas Colony team on February 1, 1923. This included the Kemerovo mines, the chemical plant, sawmills, brick kilns and machine shops. The hearts of the colonists were lifted after the trials of 1922 by this manifestation of confidence and support. As William Bender wrote to a friend in New York, Leo Goldstein, who was making preparations to sail with the first Kuzbas group of 1923:

> . . . when you arrive you will find greatly improved conditions. You will find it bearable, for the worst is over, the hardest nuts have been cracked. (*Kuzbas Bulletin* of May 7, 1923, p. 3)

That proved a true assessment. There would be many trials yet, but the colonists were beginning to feel the satisfaction of greater unity, better organization and improving production. Now that they would have a freer hand in introducing reforms, they were eager to show the world what American techniques could achieve in Siberia.

Coal mining

Alfred Pearson must be given a large measure of the credit for the advances in productive efficiency in the mines of the Kuznetsk Basin over the next few years. He arrived with the expertise conferred by years of experience in organizing coal mines in Pennsylvania, enriched by continual study and a respect for theoretical research in his field. He had the American engineer's habit, which set him apart from the old-style Russian engineers, of going frequently to the places where the dirty work was being done and learning from his own observation and rough-handed participation about the problems to be overcome. He also had a gift for describing his unique experience in Siberia in objective, professional accounts presented to American engineers in the pages of their technical journals. In contrast to Calvert, Rutgers and Haywood, he was not particularly excited by the Bolshevik Revolution; but he *was* excited by the opportunity opened to him to mine coal from these extraordinarily rich fields of Western Siberia. His ardor for this production challenge, an admirable example of the *demiurgos,* the creative energy of the engineer, was proof against all the attempts of political leaders in the United States to put barriers between the two nations and to deny backward Russia the benefits of engineering advances already achieved by other peoples. Pearson was an exemplar of a worldwide engineering fraternity which has contributed to the advance of civilization and demonstrated its capacity to serve human needs across cultural, national and political lines of demarcation.

When the Russian managers in Kemerovo consented in the fall of 1922 to allow the Kuzbas colonists to reactivate the Vladimir shaft, Pearson and Rutgers named J. MacDonald of Roseburg, Oregon, to be mine superintendent and John Preikshas of Kempton, West Virginia, to act as mine foreman. In those first months of work, miners from the United States were kept together and concentrated in the Vladimir shaft. The miners knew this was a major test for the whole enterprise, and they threw themselves into their work with impressive results. Russian workers, who were paid according to production, began to request transfer to the Vladimir. In this modest way, so natural and inevitable in the circumstances, one of the great purposes of the Kuzbas enterprise began to be achieved. We know the identities of some of these miners brought from the United States, though unfortunately not of all. They have earned the right to be remembered with honor:

. . . Chodinis	William Lugge
. . . Falkowski	Albert Meissner
Ephriam Kentta	Alex Nemmi
Jack Kuchelski	Abraham Seigel
John Kurall	Matt Stillinovitch
John Kurall, Jr.	Oscar Wickstrom
Bany Lucien	Leo J. Wydra

The Central shaft was the most important shaft in the Kemerovo region, so when this passed to the colonists' control in February, 1923, it meant a major increase in their responsibilities and in their opportunity to attack the inertia of custom. The old managers were of course opposed to this and did what they could to prevent changes and instill doubts and skepticism in the Siberian miners. But the Miners Union was on the side of change and with strong guidance from the Siberian Revolutionary Committee undertook to utilize the presence of these foreign miners to open the eyes and the minds of the local population to the long-range advantage of doing their jobs in new ways. The arrival of the foreigners had brought some trauma to Kemerovo, including an inevitable anxiety as to what the unknown changes in methods still to come might do to the security and the prospects of individual workers and their families. The Miners Union, under pressure from an advanced political leadership, became an ally in the implementation of American views on production strategy. This was a major factor in overcoming worker resistance to changes in their work habits.

One change was to reduce the area of the face being worked by each artel group. This permitted reduction in the number of workers in each group and consequently eliminated much of the suspicion on the part of each man that others were loafing at his expense. Output per worker was doubled, according to Pearson, wherever this change was introduced.

A second change involved the hours of operation. The custom was to cover the twenty-four-hour day with the working force divided into four shifts of six hours each. Pearson went to three shifts of six hours each with a two hour interval between them. This also produced a big gain in output per man because it allowed the clearing of powder smoke before each shift began to work.

Another change increased the efficiency of hauling the coal out of the mines by tripling the capacity of each of the wagons running on 22-inch gauge rails. Broadening the gauge would have entailed a reconstruction of the shafts, but each wagon could be lengthened and the existing rails replaced by heavier steel of the same gauge. This resulted in a big saving in transport costs. To feed coal into these larger cars, new hoists and cages were installed drawn by greater electric power.

The traditional hand-held oil lamps which had always been used by the Russian miners were cumbersome, inconvenient and, in the view of the Americans, dangerous because of the risk of gas accumulation in work areas. When they were replaced by electric cap lamps brought from the United States, the mine foreman observed an improvement in efficiency which he estimated at 20%. Electric lighting was strengthened at various points in the mine where good visibility was especially important to a smooth operation. Two large mine pumps and two air ventilating fans were installed.

The old Russian system of accounting seemed to employ many more office workers than Pearson had found necessary in similar operations in the United States, yet they seldom provided him with the data he needed to estimate cost efficiency. Rutgers and Pearson with the aid of Frank Kennell and Wallace Douglas began a campaign to penetrate the fog surrounding the Russian accounts, change the system to accord more closely with American practices and reduce the number of personnel employed in the accounting department. This lowered administrative costs while output from the mines was increasing and added to an impressive improvement in output per worker employed.

Summarizing the results of these and other changes over the two years since Americans took control of the Central mine, Pearson reported in 1925 that output had increased from 1/10th of a ton to one ton per worker employed. (*Coal Age,* vol. 28, no. 22, November 26, 1925, p. 725). There is independent confirmation of improving productivity in the Kemerovo mines contained in the report of the Council of Labor and Defense following an investigation carried out in 1924 by one of its commissions. The purpose of this investigation was to compare results obtained by the Americans in Kemerovo with those at mines in the Southern Region, especially Kolchugina, where the former administration (the Kuzbas Trust) was still in charge. This comparison would be used as the basis for a decision on expanding the jurisdiction of the Colony into the Southern Region.

The Chairman of the CLD commission was Rastopchin from the People's Commissariat of the Workers and Peasants Inspection. It included a representative from the Siberian Revolutionary Committee (Fomichev), a representative of the Siberian Union of Miners who was a Communist with much experience in the Kuzbas mines, and several specialist engineers from various Moscow organizations. Testimony was heard from critics of the Rutgers–Pearson regime, some of it from engineers who had formerly worked at the Kemerovo enterprise in the days when it was owned and operated by Kopikus. A representative of the Planning Commission, where there had always been some opposition to the granting of concessions to the Kuzbas Colony, was perceived by Rutgers to be lined up against him. The Kuzbas Trust administration (which included the Communist, Bazhanov) of course gave testimony justifying its own practices in preference to those being introduced at Kemerovo. Rutgers and Pearson were accused of being despotic in their handling of Russian workers. Doubts were also expressed that they could convert any of the mines in the Kuznetsk Basin into profitable enterprises for the Soviet economy. Rutgers was the principal spokesman for the Colony. Support from the Miners Union representative was a crucial element in defense against the charges of despotism. This support was undoubtedly due in part to the solid human relationship that had developed between the Siberian miners and their fellow miners from the Colony.

The commission was divided between a political nucleus which wanted Rutgers and Pearson to succeed in introducing radical reforms and the more conservative technical specialists whose ways were being examined and criticized in the light of foreign experience. The investigation produced a strong vindication for Rutgers and Pearson. A majority on the commission, including the chairman, Rastopchin, reported that the comparison made between the Autonomous Industrial Colony Kuzbas (AICK) and the Kuzbas Trust gave superiority to the former in productivity, earnings of the miners, financial position and supplies on hand. It concluded that AICK had succeeded in creating a viable economic organization and conditions for further successful work. It cited achievements in increasing productivity of labor, in rationalizing the organization of work and in reconstructing the administrative apparatus. It recommended handing over control of the mines of the Southern Region and the Guriev foundry to AICK (as Rutgers had requested).

This was only a recommendation from the commission majority, and the Council of Labor and Defense itself was urged by some to reject the conclusions as being politically motivated in the face of contrary views held by the specialist members of the commission. The CLD to resolve this challenge named another commission comprised of Kuibyshev, Krzhizhanovsky and Rudzutak. This review was taking place some nine months after the death of Lenin, a period when it was particularly difficult to find a clear consensus on such questions within the Soviet Government.

On November 12, 1924, the CLD made its decision approving the Rastopchin report and the recommended extension of AICK's authority. The acquisition of the Kolchugina mine and the Guriev foundry would take effect on January 1, 1925. The CLD delegated to a committee of three full authority to make decisions on any questions raised by the Colony administration. These three were:

Semyon Shvarts of the Central Committee of the Communist Party

G. Krzhizhanovsky of the Planning Commission

Yu. Piatakov of the Council of Labor and Defense.

As coal production increased, disposal of the output became a problem. This was aggravated by a reduction in the number of trains moving on the Trans–Siberian Railway in 1923. There were periods when piles of coal accumulated at the rail head in Kemerovo while Rutgers or someone else in the Colony administration (particularly Simon Hahn, Supply Officer, who daily felt the Colony's need for revenues) searched the region for customers in the free market. The Kuzbas office in Moscow sought to place contracts for this increasing output with other agencies of the Soviet Government. The problem was alleviated when the Kemerovo chemical factory began operating and receiving coal from the mine for conversion to coke. Then followed disputes with managers of the steel mills in the Urals over pricing and quality of Kemerovo coke. Rutgers suspected that the haggling was in part motivated by a desire in the Nadezhdinsk old guard to feed doubts as to the competence and efficiency of the AICK enterprise in Kemerovo.

In July 1925, after devoting several months to reorganizing production at the mines in the Southern Region, Pearson returned to the United States. He was replaced by W. J. Powell, who was no less effective than Pearson as chief mining engineer.

Completion of the chemical factory

The chemical factory on the left bank of the river formed an impressive group of eight large brick and concrete buildings surrounded by numerous smaller auxiliary buildings. The Siberian Revolutionary Committee cherished a hope, which time brought to fruition, that this would be only the first plant in a great Kuznetsk Basin industrial complex. The immediate necessity was to complete the chemical plant and get it into production. That was a complex task in the conditions prevailing in Siberia and Russia in the early twenties. Machinery was needed together with a variety of materials which would have to be imported. Also it was found that the design of some of the buildings had to be changed in order to accommodate the only type of machinery available. Work was made more difficult by a lack of blueprints. Some of these were ultimately found in April, 1923, in the possession of Angevich, former director of the Kuzbas Trust. They had been given to him a year earlier for safe-keeping by a Russian engineer, Lochansky, who was departing for work in another region. Further search turned up more blueprints in a private house previously occupied by Lochansky. Rutgers suspected motives of obstruction amounting to sabotage were at work against completion of the factory. Sand was found in the bearings of two of the major pieces of machinery. Fortunately the discovery was made before they were set in operation, so no permanent damage was done.

Dr. William H. Mahler, a member of the first group of colonists from the United States, became chief engineer of the chemical plant. He was a graduate of the University of Vienna with experience in Switzerland and Germany as well as in the United States. After studying the situation at the Kemerovo plant for a few months he departed for Germany in October, 1922, with sufficient foreign exchange at his command from Soviet credits to purchase machinery and supplies. Fortunately his expertise was commensurate with this responsibility. He spent seven months examining German machinery, laboratory equipment and chemical supplies which would be needed to make the factory productive. He also recruited several German engineers to join him in Kemerovo, adding to the international character of the enterprise. Among these were E. S. Schmidt from Essen, Engineer Orman and Engineer Stommel, a coke oven specialist.

It was late in 1923 before most of the German purchases reached Kemerovo. Some of the delay was due to exasperating bureaucratic entanglements at the Russian frontier. As Lenin had stated at a session of the Third International in 1922 in one of his last speeches:

> The State apparatus is not yet fully organized, and the former officials are deliberately or unconsciously interfering with its work.

In the meantime William Bender, superintendent of electrical power stations, and his assistant, John C. Tuchelski, were installing electrical equipment at the chemical plant and placing an electrical workshop in the west bank power plant. High tension wires were strung across the Tom River, tying the two electrical systems together.

The resourceful Supply Officer, Simon Hahn, became a hero when he procured from a Russian warehouse in Vladivostok a second turbo-generator for the chemical plant. This generator had been purchased in the United States by the tsarist government and loaded onto a Russian freighter. The ship was torpedoed during World War I and sank near Vladivostok. In 1922 the ship was raised and everything that seemed worth saving brought ashore. The turbo-generator rusted away in a warehouse until Hahn heard of it and arranged shipment to Kemerovo. There it was scoured, placed in running order, and saluted as "born again from the waves."

To Rutgers this was joyful news. There would now be a surplus of electric power, making it possible to provide electricity to the surrounding villages. Poles and insulators were mounted and wire strung across the countryside. Lights were installed in peasant huts in a symbolic and epoch-making operation. The work-brigade director demonstrated how *bliny* (pancakes) might be fried on a grill. When he plugged in an iron and pressed a wrinkled shirt, women gasped. On the following Sunday he returned to a village to find the lights still burning in daylight. "Why?" "We're afraid they might not come back on." He then showed them how the electricity could be turned off, and on again.

Many problems had to be resolved at the chemical plant before it could be brought into operation. Rutgers listed these in a long report published in the *Kuzbas Bulletin* of November 1, 1923. In the coal-crusher building, the shaft of the main transmission line was found to be bent; it had to be removed and reset. The floors of the coking chambers had to be removed in order to clean out clay, dirt and mortar that had been allowed to accumulate in passages leading to the flues. Tracks under the coal-pushers were badly out of line and had to be removed from their beds of reinforced concrete with much labor and relocated. The coke-pushers themselves had to be reconstructed because they were unusable in the coal and water tower buildings. One crucial plant employing sulphates and strong ammonia had to be changed in design to provide diluting tanks, preheaters to decrease steam consumption and a waste-gas disposal system, all of which had to be constructed and installed by the mechanical engineering crews. Rutgers's summary of this aspect of his difficulties stated:

> Upon investigation it was soon discovered that the chemical plant was in a terrible state of neglect and that serious defects had to be repaired and new designs made. The presumption that the plant was practically ready to run proved preposterous. . . .

By the beginning of 1924 enough progress had been made in overcoming these difficulties to fix a firm date for the firing-up of the plant. This was set for March 2, 1924, a day on which the colonists celebrated their achievement with a satisfaction made still sweeter by the assurance that they were noted and appreciated in far-flung places. Kotlarenko, having traveled from Moscow as representative of the Soviet Government, gave a speech full of praise for the "foreign workers". There were speeches by representatives of the Siberian Revolutionary Committee and greetings from the secretariat of the Third International, from Tom Barker in New York, from Tom Mann in London and from Communist parties in the United States, Germany and the Netherlands. A parade came marching across the frozen river from the mine side, bands playing and red banners waving against an all-enveloping whiteness. On top of the coke ovens stood Dr. Mahler and his assistants, N. Kishor, I. Goldfein, Schmidt, Orman, Stommel.[9] The dramatic moment of the day came when the heavy door was pushed open and in a burst of music and applause the flaming coke poured forth. A cry went up and was repeated again and again: "Long live the little international in Siberia!"

An entry by Ruth Kennell in her diary for March 3, 1924, gives the flavor of the time:

> Last night we had a jollification dance in the dining room. All the celebrities were there and came into our room later on. They were very lively and for once we got even with our neighbors [in the Community House], who kept pounding on the walls to quiet us. Loseff, editor of *Soviet Siberia,* and three others formed a quartette; the leader was a member of the Siberian Revolutionary Committee, a grave little fellow with a light Van Dyke beard.... The other three would join him uproariously on the chorus.

The mechanical work in improving the mines and in completing the chemical plant had imposed new tasks on the machine shops that existed on both sides of the river. These received new equipment, developed new capacities and expanded their services to the local community of peasants and workers in many different lines. Thus the nucleus of an industrial center was born and grew out of this first combination of coal mining, coke manufacture and chemistry.

The alteration in the life of the community produced by these busy foreigners casting their critical eye on deeply-rooted practices was not always appreciated. A Belgian Communist, Van Dooren, was placed in charge of a machine shop. This brought him into close contact with a blacksmith shop on which he depended for forgings. To Van Dooren the productivity of the blacksmiths (local workers of many years' experience) seemed unreasonably low, and he proposed a reorganization. The blacksmiths balked, and when Van Dooren pressed the issue they deliberately reduced their output and told him to "go to the devil." Van Dooren then discovered that the smiths were stealing materials from the shop and selling it in a black market.

A meeting was called by Rutgers, and Van Dooren made his accusation. The blacksmiths retorted that he was a "troublemaker."

Suddenly a Russian worker from the electrical department, a former sailor who had taken part in the storming of the Winter Palace, leaped to his feet and shouted at the blacksmiths: "You wreckers! You saboteurs! We should throw you out of this socialist enterprise!" This little drama portrayed a typical crisis of growth and progress, not without a painful side to people who were being wrenched out of old habits. The blacksmiths were sullen for a while, but their production went up.

Colony agriculture

Not the least exciting feature of the Kuzbas concession was the right to bring under cultivation some 25,000 acres of Siberian land. Two purposes were clearly defined: (1) To enable the Colony to supply food to its own dining rooms and the townspeople of Kemerovo, and (2) To develop a model farm which would stimulate agricultural production throughout the region.

A good start on these goals took place in the summer and autumn months of 1922 under the direction of Walter J. Lemon and Jack Harper. With four tractors brought from the United States, the plowing of virgin soil began and by winter some one hundred fifty acres had been sown with rye.

With the arrival in 1923 of W. H. Kingery, who was to become manager of the farm, and Roscoe A. Fillmore, a horticulturist who took charge of the gardening department, plans took shape that proved to be a source of great satisfaction to the colonists and impressive in their execution under the eyes of Siberian peasants. Another colonist, McDowell, was a principal assistant.

As soon as Fillmore arrived in May, 1923, he began organizing gardening crews of women and girls from the Colony divided into two eight-hour shifts in order to take full advantage of the long hours of summer daylight. Using rudimentary tools under Fillmore's expert direction, they soon had 35 acres planted with potatoes, cabbage, cauliflower, tomatoes, beans, peas, lettuce, radishes and melons. Fillmore reported in a letter dated July 31, 1923:

> A storage cellar is being built immediately for taking care of our potatoes and vegetables. This fall we hope to have our ground prepared for next spring, and this year's cultivation will mean a far better chance for gardening another year. Virgin prairie is poor for gardening the first year or two.

In the spring of 1923 a large shipment of agricultural equipment and supplies, valued at approximately $25,000, was shipped from New York. This included more tractors and plows, harrows, grain binders, 1,500 bushels of wheat for sowing, and vegetable seeds for 100 acres of truck garden. By winter of that year the first crop of rye had been harvested and another 800 acres sown to wheat, rye, millet and lentils. The Secretary of the Kemerovo District Committee of the Communist Party congratulated Rutgers on the farm's progress and told him that it was already having an effect on the local peasants. Many were expressing the hope that the creation of communes would lead to the introduction of American techniques and equipment in their own cultivation. Over the next few years the Kuzbas demonstration of advanced agricultural technology in Siberian conditions helped Soviet authorities in their campaign to increase production by combining acreage into units large enough to justify the allocation of labor-saving machinery.

The Kuzbas farm enterprise was divided into three units. The largest of these, "the big farm" of about 16,000 acres, was located 30 miles east of Kemerovo. This was devoted to grain fields and to pasture for livestock raised for meat. To the west of Kemerovo at a distance of about five miles a dairy farm of approximately 7,000 acres was created. From time to time breeding stock for the improvement of herds was imported from abroad. A vegetable garden of 2,000 acres on the right bank of the Tom near the mine kept the kitchens of the Colony supplied with a variety of vegetables. This "mine farm", as it was called, was also used to grow hay and grain for the 300 horses employed about the mine. A few milk cows were maintained there to supply fresh milk to the mine-side residents, sometimes cut off from the left bank by dangerous ice in a freezing or thawing river or by bad weather. Colony poultry, developed from chicks brought to Kemerovo in 1922 by C. Van Erickson from Seattle, were also located at the mine farm.

By the year 1924 the Colony was able to feed itself from these three farm entities with a growing surplus to be sold in village markets. Salt and some sugar could be purchased locally, but for coffee, tea, chocolate and tobacco the colonists continued to be dependent on shipments from friends and relatives. The search for good cooks to work in the community dining halls, one on each side of the river, could never produce satisfaction to all the colonists because of the diversity of nationalities, tastes and customs to be satisfied. But the Colony dietician, Kevah Ortt, was skilled and resourceful, and she directed the food department with almost unanimous approval. There was a rivalry between the two kitchens beneficial to the clients of both. Mrs. Wyranen, who arrived in 1923 and became chief cook on the left bank, is mentioned in letters from colonists as an expert who set a new standard. The Colony had its own bakery, though many of the colonists came to prefer the coarse black bread to which they were entitled as part of their ration as workers (the *pyok*). It was considered to be more nutritious, and to some tastes it was more appealing.

The commissary was supported financially by the contribution of sixty percent of wages by each of the colonists who received wages, plus some subsidy out of a general fund at the Colony's disposal due to revenues from its industrial activities. Mrs. Alfred Pearson took the lead in volunteering to work in one of the kitchens. This led to a Colony decision that all wives who were not employed in a work category should contribute work in the kitchens. This was resisted by some and led especially to bitter feelings between Mrs. Pearson and Mrs. Hahn, wife of the Supply Officer. With irrefutable logic, the women thus conscripted demanded to know why they alone should work without receiving wages. They were then placed in a work category and paid wages like other workers.

Gradually the number of families with their own cooking facilities increased and with this a general desire for more flexibility in eating arrangements. Exemptions from the sixty percent contribution and from obligatory paid work in the community kitchens multiplied and finally in 1925, the dining rooms were being run like restaurants, with customers paying for the meals they chose to consume.

Colony life

By the end of 1923 the housing situation had improved considerably due to several factors. Many conscripted workers who had been brought to Kemerovo during the war period returned to their peasant homes. The "company town" surrounding the Kemerovo mines was enlarged by a substantial number of log cabins (at least ten, according to Rutgers) transported from the Altai region where the mines were not being worked and the cabins were standing vacant. Finally, construction was going on continually under the direction of colonist Cother. The two-story Community House was completed in 1923. Fifteen houses, each equipped to house four families, were built near the Central shaft. Space in the Stone House became available as some Russian specialists departed and some Americans elected to move into other quarters. The Pearsons by the end of 1923 were living in a "log bungalow located in the woods near the Stone House" (*Kuzbas Bulletin*, December 1, 1923, p. 4). Ruth Kennell, after her husband's departure for the United States, chose to move into the Community House, where she shared a room with the Colony schoolteacher, Elsa Mehlmann. Kevah Ortt, on the other hand, moved out of the Community House in order to take up residence in a log cabin, dubbed "Kevah's Nest", that she helped construct in a nearby forest. The "landlord" who allocated the space and escorted new arrivals to their quarters was the colonist Graeper, who bore the title "Housing Commissar." Colonists paid no rent.

One large room of the Community House became a school for those children in the Colony who did not know sufficient Russian to attend the Kemerovo schools. With the arrival of Elsa Mehlmann from Berkeley, California, in 1923, the schoolroom of some 45 students of various ages and nationalities passed to the charge of an experienced teacher with a California credential. Prior to that time school had been hit or miss under the direction of Amy Schechter, who never succeeded in gaining the confidence of parents in her ability to handle responsibility for such a vital activity in Colony life. Perhaps feeling defeated by her assignment, Schechter abandoned the Colony to return to the United States about the time of Mehlmann's arrival. The generally improving morale in the Colony made it a good moment for a new beginning under competent direction in the classroom. There seems to be no question that Mehlmann did excellent work during the two years of her contract. One colonist, the machinist Woomer from Pittsburgh, sent for his 16-year-old son to join him in what to some anyway had become a satisfying life with a promising future to be commended to a new generation. Woomer wrote that he wanted to prepare his son to "take my place when I am through."

Some of the Colony children attended Russian schools, where their acquisition of the language was rapid. These children increased the contacts and interaction between Colony and local residents. One of them was Anna Preikshas, the 12-year-old daughter of John Preikshas, mine foreman. In January, 1923, she wrote to her friends in West Virginia:

> I go to Russian school every day and can write and read in Russian. I cannot speak very much Russian yet, but the Colony is holding night classes to teach everyone the language. Papa is teaching how to sing in Russian. . . .
>
> In Summer it is warm and beautiful. We go swimming, fishing, boating and hunting. In Winter we are sleighing, skating, etc. Bring your skates when you come. . . .
>
> Bring along some pigeons and a few parrots. And papa needs two steel fishing rods about 10 feet long and plenty of hooks, size 7. (*Kuzbas Bulletin*, April 1, 1923, p. 5)

With fishing rods and "plenty of hooks" in the summer and skates in the wintertime colonists of all ages enjoyed a year-around variety of recreation afforded by the Tom River. There was boating and swimming, boat fishing, bank fishing, and ice fishing. Many liked hiking in the pine forests, hunting in the Siberian *taiga* or sleigh rides behind a troika of horses across the winter snow. It became a custom with some of the colonists to travel to Shcheglovsk, capital of the district, for shopping in the bazaar and sightseeing. Sometimes there were visits by Americans to Siberian homes. There were frequent band concerts for the general public, with performances by both Colony and Kemerovo groups and often ending with accordian music played by the Tatars.

Temperatures dropped forty degrees below zero in the winter, but by day there was usually a feeble sun and always plenty of coal for the big brick stoves in the corner of every room. Before winter set in, Simon Hahn would issue to everyone their *shubas* (long sheepskin coats), black astrakhan caps and felt boots. Winter had the advantage of easy communication from one side of the river to the other across the ice.

The most important holiday of the year was May 1st. There was no longer any safe crossing on the river ice by that season, so separate parades and celebrations were held on the mine and the factory sides. The fire department wagons carrying their barrels of water, hoses, hooks and ladders were freshly painted; the horses had bells, with bows of red paper in their forelocks. A mounted militia headed parades to the assembly places, where leading Communists and trade unionists from town and Colony made appropriate speeches. When it was Rutgers speaking, Bronka Kornblitt translated it into Russian with great fervor. After each speech the band played a few strains of *The International*. After the ceremony a lunch would be served in the Community House to several hundred Kemerovo children and at night a dinner in honor of all the local Heroes of Labor.

The colonists organized baseball, football and soccer teams. An old Orthodox church on the mine side had been converted into a gymnasium for exercise and indoor sports. There were frequent matches between Colony and Russian soccer teams. In one of these the Colony hosted a team from an artillery encampment near Topki. The match was followed by a dinner in the Community House, toasts with kvass (a fermented drink of black bread and malt), songs and dance. Before departing, the soldiers rose and shouted in unison: "Spaseebo!" (Many thanks!)

Ruth Kennell

No one contributed more to the morale of the colony than Ruth Kennell. She evolved in her political views during the troubles of 1922 from an initial identification with the IWW partisans to an acceptance of the Rutgers reforms and the pragmatic Colony regime resulting from the new Agreement. She had been happy to escape the demands of a narrow conventional domesticity in her California life. She met the Siberian challenge with an exhilarated sense of liberation and a determination to make a new life for herself in revolutionary Russia. She was not grieved to bid farewell to her husband as he returned to the United States in early 1923, still denouncing the Rutgers revisions. She declined to join him and instead threw herself into her work for the Colony. She organized a library, located at first in a trade union club and later more conveniently on the top floor of the Colony's main administration building. It was supplied with technical books and recreational reading sent from the United States. Her office–library became an unofficial headquarters, a kind of nerve center of Colony life where mail was received and delivered. Rutgers respected and appreciated her importance and in turn won her confidence and support. She had talents as an actress and director of plays, and these she used to enrich life in Kemerovo with entertainment in the two theaters by Colony casts of amateur actors performing plays by George Bernard Shaw and others.

When Ruth Kennell completed her two-year contract at Kemerovo she moved to Moscow where on the recommendation of Rutgers she obtained work as a librarian in the secretariat of the Communist International. At Rutgers's request she returned to Kemerovo in December, 1924, to assist in a reorganization of the planning department files. In the meantime her husband had returned to Russia with their three-year-old son, James (named after an IWW leader, James Malley). Ruth was still not willing to revive their marriage. Frank Kennell became a teacher of English in Tomsk; Ruth returned to Moscow to resume her work at the secretariat. The youngster James was with his mother for a while in Moscow and then traveled with Frank to London where he was placed in the care of Frank's mother.

Ruth Kennell has described her anguish at the times of these several separations from her first child. When a choice had to be made, the claims and the attraction of life and work in the Soviet Republic were stronger with her than a mother's desire for possession of her child. In 1927 and 1928 Ruth Kennell traveled about Russia for several weeks with Theodore Dreiser as his secretary and interpreter. He later expressed a high regard and affection for her, and this is evident in the biography of her under the name, "Ernita", which he included in one of his books, *A Gallery of Women*. Ruth Kennell also wrote about Dreiser in one of her books, *Theodore Dreiser and the Soviet Union, 1927–1945: First Hand Chronicle* (New York: International Publishers, 1969). In it she appears as a champion of Soviet progress against the complaints and the strictures of the traveling American novelist. In later years she believed she had been a factor in bringing Dreiser to a warmer appreciation of the Russian revolution and to his later decision to join the Communist Party of the United States.

Rutgers needs rest

We have followed Ruth Kennell into some of her later experiences. Now let us return to the Kemerovo of 1923. The assumption of control of the mine and the chemical factory by AICK did not put an end to resistance on the part of Russian technicians to these foreign intruders. The hostile campaign of the *spetsy* made much use of the feeling of insecurity generated by the reorganization of the mine and the increasing *per capita* output. The work force in the mine was being reduced as a result of American methods, and everything the Communist Party and the labor unions could do to justify these reforms and soften their effects on workers was not enough to eliminate undercurrents of anxiety and resentment.

In the early summer of 1923 a tragedy occurred which created new material for a campaign of whispers against the presence and activities of the Colony of foreigners. Two Dutch engineers brought to the Colony by Rutgers, A. Baars and Anton Struik, designed a boat and cable system which promised to speed up transport across the river in the ice-free months. It consisted of a cable strung across the river high enough to permit the passage of boats beneath it. To this cable a boat for passengers was secured by a sliding ring. By using the boat's rudder to steer the boat at an angle to the current of the river, a combination of forces on the boat was generated to propel it rapidly across the river without any other motor power. Skill was required of the helmsman, especially when the river currents were swift as in the early summer. The new system was inaugurated on May 19, 1923. For a half day the innovation was a source of delight, and apparently the helmsman made the operation look easy. In the afternoon a group of impatient passengers decided to make the trip without him. In midstream the boat capsized and 18 people were drowned. Only one of the victims, Joseph Marta-lich, was a Colony member, so the tragedy had struck mainly Russian households.

It was easy to turn this grief against the colonists. They were not only destroying job security; they were creating hazards to the lives of the whole community. Rutgers ordered a full investigation, placing it in the hands of labor unions that were headed by local workers. Their conclusion exonerated all colonists of blame for the accident. The investigation produced testimony of the heroism of one colonist, J. MacDonald, whose quick and courageous action had saved several lives. The investigation served to mitigate but not to eliminate uneasy feelings against "the Americans." The town itself was divided on many questions in that difficult period of reconstruction and reorientation, so despite support from the unions, the Colony continued to be vulnerable to campaigns of rumor and slander.

The death of Lenin on January 21, 1924, brought a heavy sorrow to Kemerovo and the Colony. Funeral services were held simultaneously a few days later all across Russia at two o'clock in the afternoon, Moscow time. The hour was dark in Kemerovo, where the time was six in the evening. A huge and solemn crowd, many weeping, assembled in a park as a band played again and again the slow strains of a Russian dirge. Miners wore their working caps equipped with electric lights on the forehead. There were speeches of mourning in the bitter cold. At the appointed hour mine and factory whistles blew a final salute to the fallen leader, and an Honor Guard fired rifles into the sky.

The death of Lenin was a severe blow to Rutgers. We have seen how much importance he attached to Lenin's personal support for the Kuzbas project. Now a period of interregnum had begun in Russia in which the enemies of AICK would have a freer hand while its champions in Moscow would be preoccupied with even larger problems. The struggle in the year 1924 with the Kuzbas Coal Trust over extension of AICK authority to the Southern Region left Rutgers exhausted and even depressed, despite the decision of the Council of Labor and Defense in the Colony's favor. He wrote to his wife in December, 1924, that "continuing this work is like suicide for me" (Trincher, 1967, 156). The marked deterioration in his health shocked his wife, who saw him after an interval of several months. She began a campaign to extricate him from burdens she believed he was no longer able to carry. She departed with their children for the Netherlands with a promise from Rutgers that he would soon join them for some months of rest.

Bronka Kornblitt

A major reason for Rutgers's depression at the end of 1924 was the serious illness of Bronka Kornblitt. This Polish Communist was in fact Rutgers's chief deputy, probably the first woman in history to fill the role of a leading administrator in heavy industry. In the fall of 1924, she led a team from Kemerovo on a survey of the facilities in the Southern Region which were to be taken over by

AICK. This included an attempt with the aid of the bookkeeper, Douglas, to penetrate the true state of the Kuzbas Trust accounts. Kornblitt reported their findings in letters to Rutgers. The atmosphere in which they worked was of course hostile, and the investigation was made doubly burdensome by the deliberate efforts of the Trust *spetsy* to hide reality in obscurity and confusion. Among other heavy debts discovered (which AICK would have to assume) were unpaid wages of workers. Under the strain of these travels, labors and anxiety for the future of AICK, Kornblitt fell ill with a recurrence of tuberculosis. She lay in bed with a fever and a cough that brought blood from her lung. Rutgers sent her to a hospital in Tomsk where a doctor advised that her condition was serious and that she would be unable to return to work soon. He ordered her transferred to a sanatorium for tuberculosis patients at Yalta in the Crimean peninsula on the Black Sea. She was there during the spring of 1925 while Rutgers was attempting to arrange affairs in Kemerovo in such a way as to permit his own departure for the Netherlands to rest for a few months.

With the aid of the Siberian Revolutionary Committee Rutgers obtained a loan from a bank that allowed AICK to pay back-wages due in the Southern Region and also to raise wages of the Southern miners to the Kemerovo level. Engineer Kalnin was sent from Novo–Nikolaevsk to substitute for Rutgers in Kemerovo during his leave of absence, which began in March, 1925.

There were important problems to be dealt with in Moscow; for example, the price to be paid by Ural industries for Kemerovo coke, so that Rutgers did not arrive in the Netherlands to join his family in Amersfort until May, 1925.

Six days after his arrival he received a telegram from Moscow advising that the head physician at Yalta reported Bronka Kornblitt's condition to be hopeless. Rutgers quickly changed his own plans and traveled to Yalta. Undoubtedly, as Rutgers reported to his daughter, Bronka was greatly lifted by his arrival and had a few days of joy. She wanted to hear all about people and events at Kemerovo, Novo–Nikolaevsk and Moscow, about the Southern Region and about Rutgers's plans for developing the Telbess. He was with her for three weeks before she died in the early days of June, 1925. An obituary appeared in *Izvestia* in Moscow on June 13th.

Rutgers arranged her burial in Yalta with a monument at her grave reading: "Here lies a will of iron and a heart of gold."

Every colonist felt the blow of her death. Anton Struik wrote to his brother that by her energy and perseverance she had a decisive influence on Rutgers and on the Kuzbas enterprise and that her death was "a great loss." Other colonists described her as at times unrestrained but always responsive; she was one who forgot herself in her work. Ruth Kennell wrote: "She was really clever and of a frail, hectic beauty, and although she had only one lung she never spared herself in work for Kuzbas." Perhaps the most vivid description came from the American doctor, Helen Wilson, who was Colony physician from 1923 to 1925, and from Elsie Mitchell, another colonist. In their article in *Asia* (December, 1928), we read of Bronka Kornblitt:

> To the end she spent herself heroically, selflessly, passionately, burning with a feverish, neurotic, irregular flame. Her attitude toward the robust human beings who composed the Colony was scorching contempt in contrast with the Director's weary incomprehension. An appeal to her was like invoking the lightning.

Truly, hers was an enviable life, the stuff of tragedy. With her frail body and strong character she wrung from her times the chance to leave her mark on this historic enterprise, in which she passionately believed and effectively helped to advance.

9

THE TRANSITION TO SOVIET ECONOMY

By 1925 a vigorous campaign under the impulse of the central government in Moscow to "increase labor productivity" and "lower the costs of products" was being implemented through the Communist Party in every part of the Soviet Republic. This drive to establish a "Scientific Organization of Labor" (N.O.T., from its initials in Russian) became a determining factor in the latter years of the Kuzbas Colony. There was a strong tendency under N.O.T. to make every industrial enterprise conform to certain standardized practices of cost accounting and to frown on deviations as evidence of negligence by managers. The foreign technicians who were working at Kemerovo did not believe the N.O.T. practices to be superior to their own, so there was resistance to accepting the new rules as progressive and beneficial to the Kuzbas operation. Kalnin, named to the post of Acting Director in Kemerovo when Rutgers departed for Moscow and the Netherlands in March, 1925, was a Communist who considered himself subject to the requirements of N.O.T.

Rutgers by 1925 believed that the time had come to phase out the AICK and to return all the enterprises operated by the Colony to the general economic system of the Republic. His own exhaustion and deteriorating health were factors leading him to the conclusion that he personally could no longer carry the Director's burdens; the death of Bronka Kornblitt following that of Lenin undoubtedly added other reasons for Rutgers's decision to bring his tenure to an end. The choice of Kalnin as his deputy and Acting Director, made by the Siberian Revolutionary Committee in consultation with Rutgers, was a sign that the definitive transition to Russian management was underway.

The change from Rutgers to Kalnin opened a period of anxiety for the foreigners working in Kemerovo. Many of them thought that Rutgers with his peculiar combination of gifts, connections and experience was indispensable to stability and further progress in production at the Colony enterprises. Within a few weeks Rutgers was receiving letters in Moscow from some of the colonists saying that Kalnin was hindering the work of the foreign specialists. This was undoubtedly due in part to Kalnin's introduction of the detailed requirements of N.O.T. as procedures to be studied and implemented in Kemerovo. Colonists in a general meeting passed a resolution condemning Kalnin and sent a copy to Rutgers. On April 10, 1925, Rutgers acted on these complaints by sending a telegram to the Siberian Revolutionary Committee saying that AICK should soon be transferred to the regular system of Soviet economy but that Kalnin was doing harm by trying to make the change too hurriedly. In Novo–Nikolaevsk a commission was created headed by Kosior, secretary of the Provincial Committee of the Communist Party, to study the complaints against Kalnin in Kemerovo. As a result of this investigation, Kalnin was removed (Trincher, 1967, 159–160). In effect, the commission expressed its judgment of the importance of the foreigners to Soviet aspirations by ratifying their criticisms of Kalnin. It was a vote of appreciation and confidence in the Colony.

While this investigation was taking place the Council of Labor and Defense created another commission, headed by Rastopchin, to visit the Southern Region of the Kuznetsk Basin and particularly the blast furnace at Guriev. When Rutgers learned of this commission on his return to Moscow from Yalta following the death of Bronka, he decided to return to Kemerovo to assist the commission and also help find a more satisfactory deputy and Acting Director to replace Kalnin. Refreshed by his month of rest at Amersfort and Yalta, Rutgers could not let these important matters be resolved without his own personal participation.

Rutgers wanted the Acting Director to be a Russian rather than another foreigner like himself. Yet the experience with Kalnin had proven that many of the colonists, particularly the engineers and technical specialists, were jealous of what remained of their "autonomy", their exemption from meticulous control of their enterprise by Russian executors of the Scientific Organization of Labor. Letters written during this period by the Hollander, Anton Struik, chief of the drafting room in Kemerovo, recorded his misgivings over the prospect that Rutgers would remove himself from active direction of the Colony (*Een Nederlander in Siberia: Brieven Van Anton Struik*, Nijmegen, Netherlands, Socialistrese Vitgeverij Nijmegen, 1979). The Struik letters give us an insight into the final phase of Rutgers's career as Director of AICK. His last major problem was that of weaning the colonists from their dependence on him and leaving them with a minimum of trauma as they adapted to their predestined roles as functionaries in a Soviet enterprise under Russian supervision. Such a transformation was always foreseen in the Kuzbas idea, though a timetable had never been set down. Rutgers could doubtless have continued as Director as long as he wished and but for his declining health the transition might have been carried out more gradually. The discontent with Kalnin expressed by the colonists did not persuade Rutgers to prolong his own tenure. It did however lead him to support the formal creation of an advisory council of three colonists—Struik, Nemetz and Douglas—which was to be consulted faithfully by the new Acting Director, the Russian Losev, on all policies. It was a way of reassuring the colonists that their views would have a hearing as the transition proceeded.

Rutgers returned from Kemerovo to Moscow in September, 1925. The report of the Rastopchin commission on AICK's progress and plans for the Southern Region was favorable, and an increased budget for the year beginning October 1, 1925, was approved by the Council of Labor and Defense. The opening of a second battery of coke ovens at the chemical factory in 1925 increased employment, production and revenues. All the Kemerovo enterprises were now operating at a profit.

For several months Rutgers had been working on an article setting forth his views on the importance of developing the iron resources of the Telbess region. This he now completed and dispatched for publication in the magazine, *Soviet Siberia*. By the end of 1925 Rutgers was with his family again at Amersfort and from there he put in writing in letters to Foote and Kotlyarenko in Moscow his still firm decision to withdraw permanently from the Director's post in the Kuznetsk. This put the responsible authorities on notice that they would have to find someone capable of assuming the directorship fully and not merely as Rutgers's deputy as in the cases of Kalnin and Losev. When Rutgers returned to Kemerovo in February, 1926, thereby allowing Losev to return to his post in Novo–Nikolaevsk, it was understood by all that Rutgers would be turning over his responsibility to a new Russian Director as soon as one could be found with the necessary qualifications.

The man chosen by the Council of Labor and Defense was Korobkin, a member of the Communist Party, a former partisan soldier with the Red armies during the Civil War, and recently an official with management responsibilities in the Donbas coal mines. There he had developed close relations with a staff of Russian coal mining specialists, and he made it a condition on accepting his new post that they accompany him to the Kuznetsk Basin. This team had its own ideas as to how Kuzbas should be developed, and Korobkin being a man of great energy and considerable prestige, changes in policy and procedures were introduced without much concern for their effect on morale of the foreign technicians accustomed to the Rutgers regime. This period of the transition proved to be a difficult one for all concerned.

Korobkin and his staff arrived in April, 1926, and two months later Rutgers departed for the Netherlands. Letters were soon arriving from colonists complaining that Korobkin was undoing much of the good accomplished in management practices over the previous years. Rutgers reacted to these complaints by returning to Moscow in August, 1926, and taking part in creation of a new Managing Board for Kuzbas which would consist of Rutgers, Korobkin, Kotlyarenko and Struik. During those weeks in Moscow Rutgers talked to Korobkin about the problems that were arising. Rutgers then returned to the Netherlands, having decided it would be better not to visit Kemerovo under the circumstances. He was determined to see the transition accomplished, and he thought Korobkin capable of handling the task if given more time.

Unfortunately, the situation as viewed by the colonists did not seem to improve, and letters denouncing Korobkin continued to arrive at Amersfort. The complaints of Struik and Hahn were that

Korobkin allowed himself to be guided by his specialists in ways that hurt the enterprise while benefiting the specialists. They charged that the administrative apparatus was being expanded while subsidiary enterprises were being liquidated. Productivity and with it wages were falling. "Means are being squandered for the personal needs of Korobkin and his specialists from the Donbas" (Trincher, 1967, 165). There were pleas in these letters to Rutgers that he owed it to the Colony to return in person and halt the retreat.

Rutgers sent a telegram to Kuibyshev in Moscow detailing these complaints from aides whom he trusted. He now recommended that Korobkin be removed. At the end of 1926 he again returned to Moscow, where he offered to resume duties as Director in Kemerovo on condition that Korobkin be removed and a new Russian deputy named. His condition was not met, and Rutgers had to face the fact that his authority in Moscow was not sufficient to vanquish a Russian of Korobkin's standing. Rutgers then returned to Amersfort, and Korobkin proceeded to dig his own grave.

By May, 1927, the departure of foreign specialists from Kuzbas in protest against Korobkin's policies had caused the People's Commissariat of Workers and Peasants Inspection to create a commission of investigation. This led to a decision to remove Korobkin from the post, to expel him from the Communist Party and to try him on charges of abuse of power and negligence in his duties. In 1928 he was sentenced to a prison term of eight years. Some of his Russian specialists were also charged, tried and sentenced. The principal counts in these charges were that sums had been wasted and figures falsified. The commission and the tribunal concluded that Korobkin had driven out foreign specialists by his policies, to the detriment of the enterprise. In this fashion the organs of Soviet power also pronounced a judgment of appreciation in favor of the foreigners who had traveled from afar and labored hard to aid the peoples of the Soviet Republic in the task of building industry in the Kuznetsk Basin.

We have now reached the end of the history of the Autonomous Industrial Colony Kuzbas as such. Henceforth it became a history of individuals working in different Soviet enterprises. Some of the Kuzbas colonists stayed on in Kemerovo as the mines and factories became fully integrated into the Soviet economic administration.

Frank Grund had arrived in Kemerovo at the age of 20 in 1922. He worked first as a cook, then as a miner and later in construction at the chemical factory. He decided to stay on permanently. After several more years of work he was sent to the Technical Institute in Tomsk for further training. He returned to Kemerovo to continue a career that lasted into the 1970s. During World War II he helped produce coke at one of the few such plants not disrupted by the German invasion.

Ruth Kennell returned to the United States, where she wrote several children's books based on her Soviet experiences. In the early 1930s, she was Moscow correspondent for the NEA Service Newspaper Syndicate. Ruth and Frank were reunited in the United States after her assignment as an NEA correspondent. The Kuzbas years had expanded their social outlook and intensified their commitment to a better world. They worked together on a multitude of social issues and for American-Soviet friendship until Frank's death in 1970.

When Ruth Kennell visited Kemerovo in 1931 she found twenty-five colonists still working there. Among them were W. A. Warren, a construction engineer, V. Smislov, a master mechanic, and John Preikshas, mine foreman. (John's son, Eugene, worked in Siberia until retirement. He and his sister, Anna, were interviewed by this writer; see pages 7 and 10.)

In Kuznetskroy, Siberia, Kennell found several more colonists, among them V. Steinhardt and Charles Schwartz. The latter had been one of the first Americans to arrive at Kemerovo in 1921. He left Kemerovo in 1926 to study in Tomsk. In 1931 he was a school administrator in Kuznetskroy.

Some colonists continued to work in the mines of Kolchugina (renamed Leninsk) and Prokopevsk. Others helped to build the Kuznetsk Metallurgy Plant. A few, among them Anton Struik, left Kemerovo to work on the Turk–Siberian Railway. In the 1930's, Struik returned to the Netherlands where he played a leading role in the struggle against the Nazis. He was taken prisoner by the Germans in 1941 and was killed in 1945 by a British air raid.

Elsa Mehlmann, the Colony schoolteacher, left Kemerovo in 1926 and traveled to Moscow where she worked for several more years as a teacher. W. H. Kingery and J. A. Tuchelski joined agricultural groups working in the Caucasus.

Bill Haywood lived the rest of his life in Moscow, always available for interviews with visiting Americans despite his declining health. Following his contributions to Kuzbas, he was active with the Russian section of the International Organization for the Relief of Revolutionary Fighters (MOPR). He made several speaking trips in the Soviet Union, telling about Tom Mooney, Warren Billings and other U.S. labor prisoners and their struggles, a cause always close to his heart. When he died in 1928, half his ashes were buried in the Kremlin wall; the other half, in accordance with his wishes, were placed in the Waldheim cemetery in Chicago near the graves of martyrs hanged as a consequence of the Haymarket riot.

Herbert Calvert, following his departure from the New York office in 1923, lived a long life as a part-time salesman and an advocate of socialist causes. He died in Los Angeles in 1981, still proud of the part he had played in the founding of the Kuzbas Colony. He and the author of this account had fixed a date for an interview at Calvert's home; a date, unfortunately, that followed his death by a few days.

Rutgers maintained close relations with Soviet leaders throughout his life. He died in 1961. His sons worked from time to time as civil engineers on Soviet projects. One died in Moscow during World War II. His daughter married in the Soviet Union and became a Soviet citizen. She ends her biography of her father with his judgment on the Kuzbas enterprise:

> Our experiment was a success... Our little international in Siberia created a great industrial enterprise, and all this remains and will continue to grow. We showed what the international solidarity of workers can achieve.

There had been many disappointments and a substantial reduction in the magnitude of the project as compared to the proposals of 1921. To none of the founders was it given wholly to say, "I have lived my dream". Nevertheless, it still stands as an inspiring example of American-Soviet friendship and cooperation despite many obstacles. As such, it deserves to be more widely known, to be cherished and celebrated in our own perilous times.

AGREEMENT OF THE COUNCIL OF LABOR AND DEFENSE
WITH THE INITIATORY GROUP OF AMERICAN WORKMEN

The Council of Labor and Defence of the Russian Socialist Federative soviet republic, on the one hand, and the Initiatory Group of American Workmen, represented by Comrades HAYWOOD, RUTGERS, CALVERT, BEYER, AND BARKER on the other hand, have concluded between themselves the following agreement. [10]

1) The Initiatory Group, augmented in the order indicated in paragraph 5 of the present agreement by representatives of trade unions and other organizations of American Workers, forms an Industrial Colony for the purpose of exploitation of the Nadejdinsky plant and a number of enterprises in the Kuznetsk Basin. The Colony is under direct control of the Council of Labor and Defence, and its local organs, and functions in accordance with a special statute enacted by the Council of Labor and Defence in conformity with the fundamental articles stated hereunder.

2) The Colony administers and exploits the following enterprises;

a) Nadejdinsky Plants with all the subsidiary establishments, mines, pits, forest tracts, etc. specified in accordance with a list prepared by the Ural Economic Conference.

b) Coal deposits at Kemerovo with the whole present equipment for their exploitation and with all auxiliary and similar enterprises; coke furnaces, chemical works, brick kilns, sawmills, etc., specified in accordance with a list prepared by the Siberian Revolutionary Committee.

c) Two brick kilns in the city of Tomsk.

d) One leather factory and one shoe shop in Tomsk.

e) Other enterprises in accordance with supplementary agreement with the Siberian Revolutionary Committee and corresponding organs.

3) The Colony constitutes a Soviet State enterprise whose entire output belongs to the Soviet Government.

4) The Colony shall work not less than two years and shall fulfill the following obligations:

a) To transport from America to Russia 2,800 thoroughly skilled workers and a technical staff requisite for the Kuznetsk Basin and 3,000 men for the Nadejdinsky Plant.

b) To invest one hundred dollars from each worker out of the colony's funds to purchase tools requisite for the works (this amount shall be supplementary to the sum assigned by the Government in accordance with paragraph 8) and one hundred dollars on each worker for the purchase of necessary food supply. Besides, the immigrating workers shall provide themselves at their own account with sufficient equipment and articles of domestic use.

c) To arrange for purchases of machinery and tools abroad from funds specially designated for this purpose according to clause b of this paragraph and clause a of paragraph 8.

d) Every immigrating worker shall sign a pledge on a specially provided form attached to this present agreement. (See Statute of Organization and the four pledges of Lenin reproduced in Appendix B.)

e) To carry into effect production plans which shall be mutually agreed upon by the Colony, the Ural Economic Conference, and the Siberian Revolutionary Committee, with this stipulation that the first year the productivity in respect to the Nadejdinsky Plants shall not be less than double of the program mapped out for 1922, and in respect to Kuznetsk Basin it shall not be less than double the actual output for the current year.

f) Those already occupied in the enterprises taken over by the Colony shall be further engaged in the works on equal terms with the members of the Colony, on condition that the former comply with the requirements and discipline established by the Colony, with this qualification, however, that they will be found able to do the work conformably to their qualifications and the established standards of production. In the course of time the Colony shall have the right to engage in the works Russian workmen on the condition that the latter be placed, materially and legally, on the same footing with the rest of the members of the Colony.

Note 1. Transportation of the immigrants and their luggage to the Russian border points shall be effected from the worker's own funds. Transportation from the Russian border points to places of settlement shall be paid by the Soviet Government and be expedited in the order of military movements.

Note 2. The stipulation with reference to a double increase of productivity of the enterprises, indicated in this agreement shall not be construed in the sense that it must necessarily result in an increase of the absolute number of workers; it shall be conditioned by the increase of the average output of each worker, the increase of the number of workers shall result in a corresponding increase in the general productivity of the enterprises

5) The Managing Board of the Colony shall be composed of Comrades already enumerated at the beginning of this agreement (Haywood, Rutgers, Calvert, Beyer, and Barker), and nine additional comrades representing various labor organizations of America and England, in agreement with the persons signing this agreement with S.T.O. and with final approval of the additional members by S.T.O.; the Council of Labor and Defence (S.T.O.) shall have a representative in the Managing Board of the Colony.

6) One representative from the Ural Economic Conference and one from the Siberian Revolutionary Committee shall sit accordingly in the organs of the Management of the Nadejdinsky Plants, and of the Kuznetsk Basin coal mines.

7) Members of the Colony individually and the Colony as a whole shall comply, with no exception, with all the laws of the Russian Socialist Federative Soviet Republic.

8) For organization work of the Colony the Soviet Government shall sign not over three hundred thousand dollars, on the following basis:

a) Twenty thousand dollars for an exhaustive economic study and investigation of the Nadejdinsky Plants and other enterprises.

b) Five thousand dollars for organization work abroad.

c) One hundred dollars for each immigrant worker. Not exceeding the remaining amount (275,000) dollars for the purchases abroad of agricultural machinery and other necessary inventory for working the coal mines.

Note. The Commissariat for Foreign Trade shall open a credit in America for a corresponding sum.

9) To guarantee the Colony the opportunity for expansion of the industrial enterprises and to the members of the Colony satisfactory material living conditions, the Soviet Government offers to the Colony the following:

a) Towards the spring of 1922 a sufficient quantity of ready timber logs for building homes of the immigrant workers.

b) Ten thousand dessiatins of land in Kemerovo district adapted for agricultural cultivation, in agreement with the Siberian Revolutionary Committee.

c) Fifty per cent of leather production at the plant and shoe factory over and above what shall be turned out during the production period of 1921–1922.

d) Fifty per cent of the coal output at Kemerovo over and above what shall be obtained there during the production period of 1921.

e) Fifty per cent of the Nadejdinsky Plants output over and above what shall be produced in accordance with the program mapped out for 1921–1922.

f) Production from the reserved agricultural lots in accordance with the rules decreed for Soviet Agricultural Economics attached to the enterprises.

g) Production from the brick kilns and the timber output after needs of the enterprises have been fully covered.

Note: Cutting of timber shall comply with the general plan of the economy established in this respect by the forest and land section.

h) The right of merchandise barter with peasants and others in compliance with the general rules in this regard.

Note. During the first year of operation of this present agreement the settlers will receive a corresponding number of rations in accordance with the rules applying to the supply of similar categories of native workers in enterprises which have been placed on a state commercial basis. Besides, during winter time of 1922–1923 all immigrants will be furnished with heavy coats and felt boots; during winter time of 1921–1922, the Soviet Government will deliver to the Nadejdinsky plant sixty thousand poods of flour for the workers occupied in cutting timber for 1922.

Note 2. The first party of workers not exceeding two hundred men engaged in preliminary work will be supplied with all necessary things, in accordance with a specially prepared list for this purpose.

Note 3. The aforesaid norms of granted production quotas shall be valid during the first year of work in the Colony, thereafter the norms shall be subject to revision and regulation by mutual agreement and the Government of the R.S.F.S.R., excepting in principle the right of the Colony to a sufficient quantity of the products from the production in order that it be able to realize the production programs.

10) To guarantee an uninterrupted operation of the enterprises taken over by the Colony, the Soviet Government undertakes to carry out the following obligations:

a) To furnish these enterprises, in accordance with an estimate submitted by the Colony and approved by S.T.O. through corresponding organs or directly from the centre, with circulating money medium necessary for operation of the enterprises and with indispensable articles, commodities, and things that cannot be obtained or produced in the district of the Colony's settlement. The supplying of these enterprises shall be conducted along lines established for undertakings placed on a commercial basis.

b) To furnish these enterprises with a sufficient quantity of railroad and water transportation.

c) To supply a necessary quantity of cement and cast iron in accordance with a special agreement, and on condition that the Colony increase the productivity of the Yashkinsky cement plant and Gurievsky Plant by placing there a sufficient number of its own specialists.

11) Should for any reason whatsoever either of the contracting parties—the Soviet Government or the Colony, find in the course of time a further operation of this compact disadvantageous, it shall have the right to declare a termination of the agreement. In that case the Colony shall be under the obligation to deliver to authorized agents designated by the Soviet Government in accordance with a special pact all buildings, equipment, inventory, including all which has been bought in accordance with this agreement, and that which shall be later obtained by the settlers, fully intact and in perfect order, without any compensation on the part of the Soviet Government. The latter shall be under obligation to offer to the settlers every possible means for an unobstructed conveyance and passage abroad through Russian border points, with property comprising personal belongings of the settlers, in compliance with regulations then in force with reference to exporting abroad. The Soviet Government in that case shall be under money obligation neither to the Colony as a whole nor to its individual members except the obligation which shall be decided upon through Equity Courts of the Russian Socialist Federative Soviet Republic or by the All Russian Central Executive Committee of the Russian Socialist Federative Soviet Republic.

Signed

THE CHAIRMAN OF THE COUNCIL OF LABOR AND DEFENSE

_____

MEMBERS OF THE INITIATORY GROUP:

_____

_____

_____

_____

_____

APPENDIX B

STATUTE OF ORGANIZATION AND PROVISIONS
ON THE BASIS OF THE AGREEMENT WITH THE COUNCIL
OF LABOR AND DEFENSE OF THE R.S.F.S. REPUBLIC[11]

The purpose of the Industrial Autonomous Colony Kuzbas is to run Nadez-bdinski Zavod and a number of enterprises in Kuznetsk Basin toward the end of creating a big modern industry in Soviet Russia.

The management of the Unit will be in the hands of a Managing Board of seven members, three reside in Kuzbas, three in the Urals and one in Moscow. These members will be selected by the workers in the Unit, subject to the approval of the Soviet authorities. The election will be for a term of one year, with the provision of a recall by 2/3rds of the workers, or by the Soviet Government.

The Board of Management is the highest organ of the Unit, and will be responsible to Soviet authorities. It will appoint and discharge the technical staff, which in its turn will supervise all labor, as well as act as advisor to the Board of Management. All workers in the Unit will belong to their respective industrial unions, which again will act in an advisory capacity to the Board of Management and the Technical Staff.

The Industrial Unions within the unit will constitute a part of the All-Russian organization of Professional Unions. Russian workers within the Unit shall have the same legal and material rights as the other participants from America and other countries.

The Unit will guarantee to its members insurance to cover injuries, incurred while working in the enterprises, sickness insurance, vacation, sanitary conditions, education, etc. at a standard which must, at least be equivalent to that provided by the laws and regulations pertaining to workers in State enterprises in Soviet Russia.

Any member who leaves the Unit, either of his own accord or otherwise will be answered for by the Managing Board of the Unit only.

For the time being an Organization Committee is formed and will function as a Managing Board, until at least three months, and at the most six months after the first groups arrive from America in their respective districts in Siberia and Ural. (This Committee will consist of W. D. Haywood, S. J. Rutgers, H. S. Calvert, J. H. Beyer, T. Barker, Tom Mann, N. Watkins, and seven comrades in America.) The members of this organization committee in Russia shall constitute the Managing Board in Russia. The members of the Organization Committee abroad will take care of the Unit's work in their respective countries in accordance with general instructions.

The members of the Organization Committee in America will select and appoint the necessary qualified technicians, specialists, and workers, and will as far as

Russian-American emigrants are concerned co-operate with Technical Aid to Soviet Russia. Russian-Americans shall not exceed 80% of the total. The Organization Committee shall be responsible for the purchases in Canada and the United States, for complete equipment of the emigrants and their transport.

PLEDGE

1. The Organization Committee and the emigrants collectively are responsible that only such workers come to Russia that are able and willing to endure the hardships and privations that are unavoidably connected with the reconstruction of industry in a rather backward country, emerging from years of war and counter-revolution.

2. Each member of the Unit who comes to Russia undertakes to work at his or her highest capacity in order to create the highest form of productivity, so that they will prove by deeds that the workers are more capable of operating industry than the capitalists. Each member undertakes to subordinate him or herself to the discipline of the Unit.

3. The members of the Unit pledge themselves, in case of misunderstanding, or conflict, that they will accept as final the decision of the highest Soviet authority in Russia.

4. The members of the Unit pledge themselves to take into consideration the extreme nervousness of the hungry and exhausted Russian workers and peasants, and to try by all means to avoid friction, jealousy, or misunderstandings, and to attempt by all means to establish friendly and amicable relations.

The undersigned declares that he is cognisant with the general plan for the industrial colonization of Kuzbas and Nadzhdensky Zavod and with all the above Statutes, and that he is prepared to accept all the obligations expressed therein, particularly the last four paragraphs. He is prepared to work at least two years in Soviet Russia and to pay his own traveling expenses thereto, for clothes for two years and, in addition, $100.00 or more, for necessary tools and machinery.

(Signed) Wm. D. Haywood
J. H. Beyer
Tom Barker
H. S. Calvert
S. J. Rutgers

October 22, 1921

NOTES

1. These documents, written by Ruth E. Kennell, Mellie Calvert and hundreds of others, are available at the library of the University of Oregon, Eugene, Oregon. They were gathered together and placed with the library by Ruth Kennell's surviving sons, James and David, after she died in 1977 (with the proviso that the *New World Review* or someone designated by its editor emeritus, Jessica Smith, or its editor Marilyn Bechtel, have full access to these materials for the Kuzbas story). Hereinafter, they are referred to as the "Kennell Collection."

2. In later years, Senator Borah took an active and important role in the broad movement for U.S. recognition of the Soviet Republic, which was victorious when the New Deal administration renewed diplomatic relations with the Soviet Union in 1933.

3. Foster's own experiences, especially the great steel strike (AFL) which he led in 1919, had moved his thinking away from the "revolutionary" dual union principle of the IWW. When he first read Lenin's *Left-Wing Communism, An Infantile Disorder* in late 1920, he welcomed Lenin's views as rounding out his own. Foster wrote that he was "attracted at first to the Communist Party by Lenin's stand on the trade union question. . . . Over many years, I had read far and wide among socialist, anarchist and syndicalist writers, but Lenin's masterly theoretical presentation was startlingly new and overwhelmingly convincing" (Foster 1939, 295) — Ed. note.

4. For the story behind Lenin's "Letter" and the full text, see *Lenin's Letter to American Workers*, New Outlook Publishers, 1970, New York — Ed. note.

5. By 1920, Soviet industrial production was only 1/7 of the 1913 level, with large-scale industry at only 1/8. (Y. Polyakov, Ed. 1971, 98) — Ed. note.

6. Wm. Z. Foster, who was a correspondent for the Federated (Labor) Press at the RILU Congress, describes Williams' report as "highly biased" (1952, 182). He wrote further that the Congress "elected a broad Executive Council, made up of four delegates from Soviet Russia, two each for all organizations from the larger countries, and one each for the smaller movements. The Executive Bureau consisted of seven elected members. A. Lozovsky, veteran trade unionist of Russia and France, was elected General Secretary." (1956, 273) — Ed. note.

7. Full unity of the early Communist Labor Party and the Communist Party was achieved in May, 1921. A "legal" arm (a public form to counter government repression of the Communists), the Workers Party, was formed in December, 1921. (P. Bart, Ed. 1979, 16) — Ed. note.

8. Although the Kuzbas–Nadezhdinsk project could not be fulfilled in the early 1920s, the vision of its proponents was fully justified. The first Soviet five-year plan, launched in 1929, included the Urals–Kuznetsk industrial region, with a network of subsidiary installations, and by 1932 the Ural–Kuznetsk iron and steel complex was in operation. This secure, thousand-mile wide industrial belt was a crucial productive base during the 1941–45 Great Patriotic War, far to the rear of the battlefronts.

9. See "Starting a Byproduct Coke Plant in Central Siberia" by N. Kishor and H. Kweit in *Chemical and Metalurgical Engineering,* New York, Vol. 32, number 2 of January 12, 1925. Also *New World Review,* New York, Vol. 39, number 4, Fall 1971; article by Nemmy Sparks (N. Kishor).

10. Footnote of Herbert Calvert: The Agreement has been copied exactly as written in 1921. My original copy with the Seal of the Council of Labor and Defense and Bogdanof's signature is in the Museum of the Revolution, Moscow.

11. English version carried by Calvert to the U.S. in 1921 and published in the *Kuzbas Prospectus* (New York, 1922).

BOOK REFERENCES CITED

BART, PHILIP
    1979   *Highlights of A Fighting History*, New York, International Publishers.

FOSTER, WILLIAM Z.
    1939   *Pages from A Worker's Life*, New York: International Publishers.
    1952   *History of the Communist Party of the United States*, New York: International Publishers.
    1956   *Outline History of the World Trade Union Movement*, New York: International Publishers.

HAYWOOD, WILLIAM
    [1929] 1966   *Autobiography of Big Bill Haywood*, New York: International Publishers.

LENIN, V. I.
    1918   *Letter to American Workers*, Collected Works 28:62–75, Moscow (1965): Progress Publishers. (Also see Note 4.)
    1920   *Left-Wing Communism, an Infantile Disorder*, Collected Works 31:17–104, Moscow (1966): Progress Publishers.
    1965   *Collected Works* 32:181–2 ff., Moscow: Progress Publishers.
    1965   *Sobranie Sochineniia* (Collected Works) 53:231, Moscow: Progress Publishers.
    1969   *Collected Works* 42:349, Moscow: Progress Publishers.
    1970   *Lenin on the United States*, New York: International Publishers. Also Moscow (1967): Progress Publishers.

POLYAKOV, Y.
    1971   *A Short History of Soviet Society*, Moscow: Progress Publishers

TRINCHER, G. & K.
    1967   *Rutgers*, Moscow.

INDEX

---

*Kuzbas colonists, most recruited by the founders of the project or by the American Organization Committee (AOC)